D1360584

44687

OAKLAND SCHOOLS LIBRARY
2100 Pontiac Lake Road
Pontiac, Michigan 48054

Evaluating
Instruction

LB
2823
.P63
1973

371.102
P827e

Evaluating Instruction

W. James Popham

Graduate School of Education

University of California, Los Angeles

PRENTICE-HALL, INC.

Englewood Cliffs, New Jersey

Muirhead Library
Michigan Christian College
Rochester, Michigan

Library of Congress Cataloging in Publication Data

POPHAM, W JAMES.
    Evaluating instruction.

      1. Educational surveys—Handbooks, manuals, etc.
I. Title.
LB2823.P63   371.I'02   72–8896
ISBN 0–13–292128–6
ISBN 0–13–292110–3 (pbk.)

© **1973 by Prentice-Hall, Inc.**
Englewood Cliffs, N.J.

All rights reserved. No part of this book may be reproduced in any form or by any means without permission in writing from the publisher.

10 9 8 7 6 5 4 3 2 1

Printed in the United States of America

Prentice-Hall International, Inc., *London*
Prentice-Hall of Australia, Pty. Ltd., *Sydney*
Prentice-Hall of Canada, Ltd., *Toronto*
Prentice-Hall of India Private Limited, *New Delhi*
Prentice-Hall of Japan, Inc., *Tokyo*

Contents

v

35082

Companion Audiovisual Materials

A set of filmstrip-tape instructional programs coordinated with the contents of this book is available from Vimcet Associates Inc., P.O. Box 24714, Los Angeles, California, 90024. Information regarding these materials is available upon request.

Evaluating
Instruction

Introduction

To improve educators in evaluating their instructional efforts is a current educational imperative. This book consists of six self-instruction programs, designed to be completed individually by the reader, which focus on the topic of the evaluation of instruction. The programs deal with various aspects of evaluation and provide a set of tangible competencies which can be employed by teachers or other educational personnel as they evaluate instruction.

In recent years educational evaluation has caused much discussion. Fortunately, some evaluation topics have advanced beyond mere rhetoric: a number of technical skills and constructs are now available to the educator who wishes to improve his expertise in evaluating instructional activities. After completing the six programs in this book, you will become more skilled in dealing with questions related to the evaluation of instruction, whether that instruction is confined to the classroom or occurs in other educational settings. The competencies provided by the programs should be of value to individuals who are preparing for a teaching career at any level of instruction. In addition, experienced teachers will find

1

that the topics treated in the programs bear upon many of the practical classroom concerns. In essence, then, both pre-service and inservice teachers should profit from completing the programs contained herein.

Organization of the Book

The book is organized around six self-instruction programs. The substance of these programs is briefly presented below:

CURRENT CONCEPTIONS OF EDUCATIONAL EVALU-ATION. The general notion of educational evaluation is examined in such a way that the reader acquires the ability to discriminate between four important conceptual distinctions recently used in the field of educational evaluation. More specifically, contrasts are drawn between measurement and evaluation, formative evaluation and summative evaluation, process criteria and product criteria, and evaluation as an assessment of merit versus evaluation as an aid to decision makers.

MODERN MEASUREMENT METHODS. This program examines recently introduced educational measurement techniques which are particularly useful to teachers and other educators engaged in evaluation. The principal focus of the program is on the distinction between *criterion-referenced* measurement and *norm-referenced* measurement. In addition, testing procedures involving an *item sampling* strategy are discussed.

INSTRUCTIONAL SUPERVISION: A CRITERION-REFERENCED STRATEGY. Recognizing the relationship between instructional evaluation and instructional supervision, this program describes two chief functions of an instructional supervisor who employs an outcome-focused strategy for improving the quality of a teacher's instructional efforts. Recommended activities associated with each of these two functions are treated in the program.

CONSTRUCTING TEACHING PERFORMANCE TESTS. The merits of a distinctive, new approach to evaluating a teacher's instructional proficiency are examined in this program. The measurement tactic involved is a *teaching performance test* and this program describes the attributes which effective teaching performance tests must possess. By completing the program, the reader should be able to construct such measurement devices.

USING TEACHING PERFORMANCE TESTS. After the reader has learned in the previous program how to construct a teaching performance test, this program provides him with specific suggestions for using teaching performance tests either for instructional improvement, that is, to help the teacher become better at his task, or skill assessment, that is, to evaluate the quality of a teacher's instructional activities.

ALTERNATIVE AVENUES TO EDUCATIONAL ACCOUNTABILITY. This program examines an evaluation theme of considerable current popularity, namely, educational accountability. The program distinguishes between three forms of such accountability, namely, personal, professional, and public. Advantages and disadvantages of each of these three educational accountability systems are treated.

The introduction to each program will give the explicit instructional objectives for the program. A separate answer sheet for each program is provided at the end of the book. These sheets are detachable and can probably be used more conveniently if they are removed from the book. A separate mastery test for each program is also provided at the rear of the book. These too can be detached. Finally, the correct answers to all mastery tests are given in the final section in the text.

Use of the Book

Since these programs are self-instructional, it is probable that you will be proceeding individually through each at your own pace. Incidentally, it is usually better to complete a whole program at a single sitting rather than to interrupt your work. Before beginning a particular program, locate the answer sheet for that program. Note the program's objectives, and begin reading the textual material. On the answer sheet write your responses to questions posed in the frames. After you have made the response, check the accuracy of your answer by reading further in the program. Preferably, you should respond in writing, although if you wish you may answer mentally. So that you do not inadvertently read too far and see the correct answer before making your response, wide bars like the one below have been inserted throughout the programs.

The correct answers will appear immediately following the bar. When you see such a bar, mask off the section below it until you have made your response (a heavy answer mask has been provided inside the rear cover), *then* read on to discover the accuracy of your answer. When you have completed a program, take the mastery test for that program and subsequently check your answers.

Several of the topics dealt with in these six programs are treated in more detail in the conventional nonprogramed text, *Systematic Instruction,* distributed by Prentice-Hall. Also available are related collections of self-instruction programs including *Planning an Instructional Sequence, Establishing Instructional Goals,* and *Classroom Instructional Tactics.*

When you are ready, move to the first program.

Current
Conceptions of
Educational
Evaluation

Objectives

At the conclusion of the program the reader will be able to discriminate between previously unencountered descriptions of real or fictitious educators as they engage in activities reflecting any one of the following dichotomies:

1. Measurement *versus* Evaluation
2. Formative Evaluation *versus* Summative Evaluation
3. Employing Process Criteria *versus* Employing Product Criteria
4. Evaluation as an Assessment of Merit *versus* Evaluation as an Aid to Decision Makers

Possibly the most pervasive theme in the nation's educational enterprise during the past several years revolves around the desirability of rigorously evaluating the quality of our instructional activities. We have been reminded by educators and citizens alike that those designing and operating instructional systems have an ethical responsibility to discover how well their instruction has worked. This heightened interest in educational evaluation has brought with it a concomitant increase in the number of individuals attempting to improve the quality of the evaluation enterprise itself systematically. Some of our finest educational thinkers have turned to the process of educational evaluation to make that process more productive. Some of the refinements emerging from their activities will constitute the focus of this program.

USEFUL TOOLS
FOR THE
EDUCATIONAL EVALUATOR

More specifically, four different distinctions currently made by educational evaluators will be probed in some detail. Each of these distinctions, if mastered, can prove extremely useful to a teacher or, for that matter, any educator who wishes to evaluate the quality of an instructional enterprise. At the close of the program you should be able to recognize instances in which these constructs are being employed in different ways. By mastering these current conceptions associated with educational evaluation, your own skill as an evaluator will be enhanced.

As our initial concern, we will consider the meaning of the basic term *evaluation*. For many years educators in this country have tossed the term around with almost indifferent imprecision. For some the expression referred exclusively to the grading operations wherein pupils were assigned A, B, C, etc. To others, it meant essentially the same as *measurement;* when a teacher completed a college course in tests and measurement, he felt he had also increased his understanding of evaluation. Still others thought of evaluation as experiments to discover if Method *A* was better than Method *B*. Although each of these notions of educational evaluation has been subscribed to by many, each is clearly inconsistent with the conception of educational evaluation endorsed by most educational leaders.

Let's consider the idea that educational evaluation and the grading of pupils are equivalent. Certainly when a teacher grades a pupil there is an evaluative operation present, for the teacher must decide how good the student's performance has been. Yet the phrase *educational evaluation* generally refers to evaluating an educational *enterprise,* such as an instructional sequence, not evaluating the pupils within that enterprise. True, many times an evaluator will appraise an educational enterprise by studying its effects on pupils, but in such situations it is the educational enterprise, not the learner, who is really being evaluated.

To explore this point, examine the following exercises and decide whether the teacher is engaged in grading or evaluation. Answer by Number 1 on the answer sheet by circling the word *grading* or *evaluation*.

1.
Mr. Jacobs feels that the final essay examination performance of his students reflects the quality of his instructional prowess during the semester, and thus carefully corrects each pupil's essay paper according to highly explicit criteria.

Mr. Jacobs was engaged primarily in evaluation. While he may also use the final essay exams to assign grades, his focus at the moment is on the quality of his teaching—a focus consonant with most current interpretations of what is meant by the phrase *educational evaluation.*

Another definition of evaluation less prevalently held (but also at variance with current thinking) equates educational evaluation with educational research. In particular, the confusion occurs when an experimenter attempts to demonstrate that two alternative instructional procedures are "significantly different." But note that this is essentially a description of what exists, namely, the presence or absence of a significant difference, and is not an attempt to discern whether that difference, or lack of it, is good or bad. Educational research-ers try to detect the existence of relationships between educationally relevant variables. They are typically not involved in appraising the *value* of those relationships.

Thus, is the individual in the following exercise engaged primarily in *evaluation* or in *research?* Circle your answer by Number 2 on the answer sheet.

2.
Bill Harris has been contrasting the effects of three films designed to promote positive learner attitudes toward citizens of other countries as reflected by anonymous responses to a questionnaire. His statistical analysis reveals that one film yields significantly higher attitude scores.

You should have answered *research,* for this activity is designed to detect which film yields which kind of results, not whether those results are good or bad.

Finally, a particularly widespread misconception of evaluation is that it is the same thing as measurement. Examining this

notion of evaluation will, finally, bring us to an explicit definition of educational evaluation. First, however, let's look at
educational measurement. As the term implies, measurement
involves measuring, that is, counting or enumerating so that
we can more accurately describe how large, small, long, etc.,
something is. Measurement consists of an assessment of the
current status of a phenomenon in a precise fashion. Thus,
for example, we discover how much students know about
multiplication by measuring their knowledge through the use
of an examination. If we report that certain students solve 90
percent of the problems, while other students solve only 10
percent, we have a more accurate picture of what our learners know about multiplication. Note that at no time in the
measurement operation are we obliged to make any value
judgments about the goodness or badness of the students'
performance, for measurement involves only more precise
description, not valuing regarding the phenomena thus described.

Michael Scriven, the evaluation theorist, succinctly observed
that *evaluation consists of an assessment of merit.* Educational evaluation, therefore, consists of assessments of merit
regarding educational phenomena. By *assessment of merit*
we mean the determination of worth or relative goodness of
whatever we are evaluating. For instance, educational evaluators frequently assess the merits of competing instructional
procedures. In this sense the evaluator is dealing with the
same enterprises that our educational researcher was in a
previous example. But the evaluator's job is not merely to
measure which instructional treatment yields the bigger result, but to reach a judgment regarding *how good* the results
are. To reiterate, evaluation consists of worth determination;
measurement consists of status determination.

Let's see if you can distinguish whether fictitious educators
are engaged chiefly in educational evaluation or in educational measurement. Note that we said *chiefly,* for there are
instances in which evaluators measure and in which mea-
surers evaluate. Focus on the *primary* activity in these exam-

ples. Is the educator in the following illustration engaged in *evaluation* or *measurement?* Circle the correct response by Number 3 on the answer sheet.

3.
A school counselor directs a testing program which yields for each pupil in the district an I.Q. score and comprehensive achievement scores in quantitative subjects and in verbal subjects.

This is a pretty obvious instance of measurement only; there is no assessment of merit involved.

How about the next example? Is measurement or evaluation primarily involved here? Answer by Number 4.

4.
Miss Foss calls in a district supervisor who observes her class for three consecutive days, noting the frequency with which Miss Foss permits pupil participation. Subsequently, the supervisor and Miss Foss decide she has permitted too little learner participation.

This is a tougher choice. The better answer here is evaluation, for when the supervisor and Miss Foss concluded that "too little learner participation" was present, they made an assessment of merit.

Now try this next exercise. Respond by Number 5 on the answer sheet.

5.
Norm Reffrenzd, an elementary school principal, annually determines the comparative percentile ranks (according to nationally standardized normative data) for each of his pupils in reading and

mathematics. These percentiles are made available to all the school's teachers.

Although percentiles are reported, and percentiles imply comparisons with a norm group, there is apparently no assessment of the goodness or badness of the pupils' performance in relationship to these norms. Hence you should have circled measurement, not evaluation.

Before turning to the next of our four key evaluation constructs, two important points should be noted. First, competent evaluators will generally take cognizance of *many criteria,* not just one, in reaching an assessment of merit. Thus, in evaluating two competing instructional procedures the skillful evaluator will naturally consider which procedure yields higher test scores, but he will also take into account such factors as cost, unanticipated side effects, teacher willingness to use the procedures, etc.

A second point relates to the *timing* of the evaluation. In most of the examples employed thus far the evaluator roars in near the close of a *new* instructional sequence to offer his assessment of merit. However, it is also important to appraise the worth of *extant* educational enterprises in order to decide where we should invest our educational resources. Typically, when educational evaluators assess the merits of ongoing educational operations they do so to aid in the formulation, or reformulation, of appropriate goals for that educational system. Educational evaluators have much to offer as they assess the merits of instructional enterprises at any point on a temporal continuum—*before, after,* and even *during.*

The second major distinction in the program is the distinction between *formative* and *summative evaluation.* We must again credit Michael Scriven with this useful distinction and the terms which have in the past few years become part of the common parlance of educational evaluators.

An instructional sequence may be evaluated to improve the sequence itself, in which case it is known as formative evaluation. Evaluation may also appraise the worth of a completed instructional sequence (in comparison with competing sequences), in which case it is known as summative evaluation.

This distinction is important because by contrasting these disparate roles an evaluator will discover that certain techniques are appropriate for one role and not for the other. To illustrate, the activities of a person engaged in the formative evaluation of a still fluid instructional sequence may be much more partisan than those of a summative evaluator who may bring external objectivity to his role as a comparative assessor of merit. The formative evaluator *wants* the instructional sequence he is working with to improve and can use short cut evaluation designs, small sample tryouts, and the like to help the instructional designers develop a more effective se-

FORMATIVE-PARTISAN   SUMMATIVE-NONPARTISAN

quence. Hunches regarding improvement tactics can come from scanty data.

Summative evaluators, working with finished instructional sequences, must be more circumspect in applying appraisal standards. Typically, action decisions will follow the work of the summative evaluator, for instance, buying Textbook *A* rather than Textbook *B,* or discarding an instructional plan rather than retaining it. Hence, summative evaluators frequently have recourse to randomized assignment of pupils and rigorous control group designs in their work, for such procedures permit more defensible inferences.

Let's give you some practice in distinguishing between evaluation situations which are primarily formative and those which are primarily summative. Circle the appropriate response for the following exercise beside Number 6 on the answer sheet.

6.
Members of a curriculum development project have called in an evaluation group to help them improve, by running limited field tests, the quality of some new instructional booklets they have developed.

This is a pretty clear instance of formative evaluation and really represents the classic case where an evaluator's role is to offer recommendations regarding how to improve an instructional sequence while it is still amenable to modification.

Decide in this exercise whether formative or summative evaluation is involved. Answer by Number 7.

7.
Mrs. Evans has been called on to design an evaluation project which

will permit school officials to decide whether to retain a costly enrichment program in the humanities or to replace it with a new
social science program.

You should have circled *summative* for this exercise, since
Mrs. Evans is trying to make recommendations regarding
which program should be chosen, not how to improve either
one of them. Scriven has argued that there is always a degree of real or implicit comparison whenever one engages in
summative evaluation.

Here is a final summative/formative exercise. Circle the correct response by Number 8 on the answer sheet.

8.
A school curriculum specialist is trying to reach a "go/no go" recommendation on a suggestion of the biology faculty that a new
one-week series of programmed instruction lessons on sex education be required in the district's curriculum.

Here again is an instance of summative, rather than formative, evaluation. As you acquire further technical skills associated with educational evaluation the importance of this
formative/summative distinction will become even more apparent.

Let's turn now to a third distinction which educational evaluators have recently found useful in their work, namely, the
difference between the use of *product criteria* and *process
criteria* in conducting educational evaluations. By product criterion we mean an indicator based on the learner behavior
supposedly produced as a consequence of an instructional

sequence, for example, the results of learners' performance on a test covering what they had supposedly been taught. Some writers refer to such product criteria as *extrinsic* criteria and to evaluation which employs these indicators as *payoff* evaluation.

To product or extrinsic criteria we can contrast *process* or *intrinsic* criteria, which are factors that are supposedly related to product criteria. When textbooks are evaluated positively because of internal characteristics such as readable print size or clever illustrations, the evaluator generally believes that such process criteria will be positively related to the product criterion of how well children learn from the textbooks.

Different instances of process and product criteria used by evaluators are:

extrinsic
Product Criteria

intrinsic
Process Criteria

1. Observed pupil behavior
2. Learner test scores
3. Student questionnaire responses

1. Number of books in library
2. Degrees earned by teaching staff
3. Financial expenditures on school

Some evaluators contend that it is perfectly acceptable, even desirable, to use process criteria in conducting educational evaluations, while others argue that process criteria have no role whatsoever in educational evaluations. To decide on the appropriateness of employing process criteria, you obviously need to distinguish these from product criteria. Let's give you a little practice in discriminating between these two types of criteria. Beside Number 9 on the answer sheet indicate whether the following educators are primarily using process or product criteria.

9.
A school evaluation committee decides to appraise the efficacy of a new curriculum scheme on the basis of the types of learner attitudes formed toward the subject matter (as reflected by responses to a specially devised attitude inventory).

You should have circled product, for an evaluation based on what happens to learner attitudes is clearly focused on changes in the learner and, as such, reflects payoff evaluation employing product or extrinsic criteria.

Try this exercise, circling the type of criterion used beside Number 10.

10.
A school administrator evaluates a new series of first-grade enrichment audiotape instructional materials positively because the instructional staff seems to think they are professionally produced and that they feature the best authorities in the field.

This is a pretty clear instance of the use of a process criterion. The administrator would have employed a product criterion if he attempted to find out what happened to the children who listened to the enrichment tapes.

For this exercise, answer next to Number 11 on the answer sheet. Is a process or product criterion being used?

11.
A new instructional strategy is judged positively because children are observed to smile more frequently during its conduct.

This one is a bit sticky. Probably the best answer is process rather than product, even though the focus is on the learner's behavior. The evaluators seem to be assessing the learners' behavior during the instructional process as an indicator of what might be a postinstruction product criterion, such as positive learner affect toward the instruction. On the other hand, an imposing argument could be mustered in favor of considering this a product criterion because the instructional sequence could be divided into smaller temporal units and each unit appraised in relationship to short term learner satisfaction. This illustrates the difficulty of making unequivocal distinctions in all cases. The evaluator will find the general difference between process and product criteria will prove serviceable in many situations.

The last of our four key evaluation distinctions considers a basic difference of opinion regarding the nature of the evaluation operation. In the last few years there has emerged a group of educators who wish to define educational evaluation not chiefly as assessing merit, but as supplying information to aid decision making. This point of view is best represented in the evaluation model developed by Daniel Stufflebeam and Egon Guba which is known as the CIPP (pronounced *sip*) model; it consists of (1) **C**ontext evaluation, in which an ongoing educational context is surveyed in order to aid in selecting educational goals; (2) **I**nput evaluation, in which alternative instructional treatments are surveyed; (3) **P**rocess evaluation, in which the progress of the selected treatment is monitored; and (4) **P**roduct evaluation, in which the results of the treatment are appraised. In the CIPP-type scheme an evaluator is essentially a selector and presenter of information, rather than a valuer. In general, those who offer evaluation as an aid to decision makers do just that—they aid *someone else* who makes the value judgment and subsequent decision. The CIPP evaluator, therefore, has a far more neutral orientation than his assessment of merit counterpart. Instead of making recommendations regarding which course of action should be taken, such neutralists supply a variety of data which, hopefully, illuminates a decision maker.

Is the evaluator in the next example behaving primarily in a fashion which could be characterized as aiding decision makers or as assessing merit? Circle the correct answer by Number 12 on the answer sheet.

12.
An evaluation consultant has been informed of the school district's goals and asked to suggest alternative methods of achieving them. Although he personally believes the goals are excessively conservative, he supplies considerable data regarding relevant instructional strategies.

This is a fairly clear instance of evaluation as an aid to decision makers. Although his own values suggest the district's goals are improper, the evaluator confines his activities to supplying helpful information.

Try this exercise and answer next to Number 13. Which orientation to evaluation is operative here?

13.
A school board is trying to decide which of three curriculum schemes to adopt. The district evaluation specialist supplies extensive data regarding each but, when asked directly for his own recommendation, declines to comment.

This, too, presents an instance of evaluation as an aid to decision makers and illustrates that such evaluators really do not consider it a legitimate part of their role to offer personal merit assessments. Their job is to gather and describe data so that those charged with assessing merit can do so more defensibly.

And this, of course, represents a crucial difference in the two conceptions of evaluation. Those evaluators employing the assessment of merit orientation consider these recent evaluation specialists moral eunuchs. On the other hand, the aid-to-decision-maker people think the assessment-of-merit folk clearly exceed their proper province. Educators are only now recognizing this basic difference between these two approaches to evaluation and the resulting differences in the activities of each type of evaluator. We can anticipate heavy controversy on this issue in the future.

In review, we have examined four not unrelated distinctions currently employed in the educational evaluation arena: first, the difference between measurement and evaluation; second, the difference between formative and summative evaluation; third, the difference between evaluation using process and product criteria; and fourth, the difference between evaluation as an assessment of merit and evaluation as an aid to decision makers. Every educator, from classroom teacher to state school chief, should be conversant with these and other advanced evaluation constructs, for clearly we should all be concerned with devising and implementing the most enlightened evaluations possible.

Modern
Measurement
Methods

Objectives

This program is designed to provide the reader with a set of skills stemming from recent advances in the field of educational measurement. More specifically, having completed the program, the learner will be able to:

1. Describe the principal purpose of (a) criterion-referenced testing and (b) norm-referenced testing.
2. Identify whether selected measurement operations are more appropriate for criterion-referenced or norm-referenced testing.
3. Properly classify descriptions of measurement devices as either criterion-referenced or norm-referenced.
4. Distinguish between measurement situations which require criterion-referenced or norm-referenced measures.
5. Describe the basic procedure, as presented in the program, for constituting tests by item sampling.

A persistent feature of the twentieth century has been the phenomenon of change. Education, of course, is an area in which modifications have occurred in recent years. But, as usual, leading edge changes in a field are slow to reach all practitioners. The area of educational measurement exemplifies this communication lag. In the past few years measurement experts have evolved markedly different approaches to important testing practices. These approaches vary considerably from the customary measurement procedures used by educators. It seems only reasonable that those individuals involved in educational measurement, including most school personnel, would wish to consider the implications of these new procedures. Accordingly, this program will examine two important departures in modern measurement methods: first, *criterion-referenced* versus *norm-referenced* testing, and, second, *item sampling*.

Let's initially distinguish between two purposes for which educators commonly use measuring devices. The basic difference between these two purposes has given rise to the concepts of norm-referenced testing and criterion-referenced testing.

At the most basic level, norm-referenced measures ascertain an individual's performance in relationship to the performance of other individuals on the same measuring device. Because the individual is compared with some normative group such measures are described as norm-referenced. Most standardized test of achievement or intellectual ability are norm-referenced measures. Criterion-referenced measures ascertain an individual's status with respect to some criterion or performance standard. Because the individual is compared with some established criterion, rather than with other individuals, these measures are described as criterion-referenced. One criterion-referenced test is the Red Cross Senior Lifesaving Test, since an individual must display certain swimming skills to pass the examination, irrespective of how well others perform on the test. Since norm-referenced measures permit comparisons among people, their primary purpose is to make decisions about *individuals*. Which pupils should be counseled to pursue higher education? Which pupils should be advised to attain vocational skills? These are the kinds of questions to be answered through the use of norm-referenced measures; many decisions regarding an individual can best be made by knowing more about the "competition," that is, by knowing how other, comparable individuals can perform.

Criterion-referenced tests make decisions both about *individuals* and *treatments*. In decisions regarding individuals, we might use a criterion-referenced test to determine whether a learner had mastered a criterion skill considered prerequisite to a new training program. In decisions regarding treatments, we might design a criterion-referenced measure which reflected a set of instructional objectives supposedly achieved by a replicable instructional sequence. By administering the criterion-referenced measure to appropriate learners who had completed the instructional sequence, we could decide the effectiveness of the sequence.

Although both norm-referenced and criterion-referenced tests are used to make decisions about individuals, there is usually a difference in the context in which each decision is made. Generally, a norm-referenced measure is employed when a degree of *selectivity* is required; for example, when there are only a few openings in a company's executive training program, the company is anxious to identify the *best* potential trainees. It is critical in such situations, therefore, that the test-measure permit *relative* comparisons among individuals. On the other hand, when we are only interested in whether an individual possesses a particular competence, and there are no constraints regarding how many individuals can possess that skill, criterion-referenced measures are suitable. Theoretically, at the close of many instructional programs we might hope that *all* learners would display *maximum* proficiency on measures reflecting the instructional objectives. In this sense, of course, criterion-referenced measures may be considered *absolute* indicators. Thus, both norm-referenced and criterion-referenced tests can be focused on decisions regarding individuals—it is the context within which these decisions are made that really produces the distinction.

NORM-REFERENCED TESTS = RELATIVE MEASURES
CRITERION-REFERENCED TESTS = ABSOLUTE MEASURES

Norm-referenced measures as well as criterion-referenced measures can be used to make decisions regarding the merits of instructional programs. Certainly, this has been a common practice as educators have evaluated their curriculum efforts on the basis of pupil performance on standardized examinations. But norm-referenced measures were really designed to "spread people out" and are best suited for that purpose.

Let's review some of these distinctions in purpose. Next to Number 1 on the answer sheet, indicate whether the following remarks are more closely associated with criterion-referenced (C) or norm-referenced (N) measurement.

1.

The primary purpose of this type of measurement is to see how close an individual approximates a given standard of performance.

You should have circled *C,* for this is a description of the chief purpose of criterion-referenced measurement.

Next to Number 2 on the answer sheet decide whether the following notion is more closely associated with criterion-referenced or norm-referenced measurement.

2.

Measures must be used to identify the top 25 sophomores for a new enrichment program in English.

The correct answer here would be *N,* for in this case the necessity to be selective requires us to use measuring devices which can discriminate among individuals. The top 25 students are "tops" in relationship to other students, not to a fixed standard.

Next to Number 3 circle the *C* or *N* for this next exercise.

3.

Should be used to assess the effectiveness of instructional sequences in promoting learner attainment of clearly explicated objectives.

Here, the answer is criterion-referenced measurement, so you should have circled *C.* Criterion-referenced tests usually provide a more accurate estimate of the degree to which instructional objectives are achieved.

Answer this exercise next to Number 4.

4.

Used to represent an individual's performance on a test in relationship to that of other individuals on the same test.

Since this describes the chief purpose of norm-referenced
testing, you should have circled the *N*.

Now, using your own words, write out a brief description of
the principal purpose of criterion-referenced measurement in
the spaces next to Number 5 on the answer sheet.

Your answer should have conveyed a notion somewhat similar to this:

> Purpose of criterion-referenced measurement: *to iden-
> tify an individual's status with respect to some criter-
> ion or performance standard.*

Once more, using your own words briefly describe the principal purpose of norm-referenced measurement in the spaces
next to Number 6 on your answer sheet.

Your answer should have conveyed an idea comparable to
this:

> Purpose of norm-references measurement: *to identify
> an individual's performance with respect to the perfor-
> mance of other individuals in the same measuring de-
> vice.*

What are the implications of these two measurement approaches for classroom teachers and other educational decision makers? We shall now examine the differences between norm- and criterion-referenced measurement with respect to item construction, item improvement, reliability, and validity.

The basic differences between item construction in a norm-referenced framework and item construction in a criterion-referenced framework is a matter of "set" on the part of the item writer. Until computers can cough forth many items per minute, someone is going to have to construct test items. The primary difference in purpose between norm-referenced and criterion-referenced measurement will usually influence the item writer to a considerable degree. "Item" here refers to any kind of procedure used to measure learner performance.

When an individual constructs items for a norm-referenced test, he tries to produce *variant* scores so that individual performances can be contrasted. As a consequence, he makes all sorts of concessions, sometimes subtle, sometimes obvious, to promote variant scores. He disdains items which are "too easy" or "too hard." He avoids multiple choice items with few alternative responses. He tries to increase the allure of wrong answer options. He does all of this to develop a test which will produce different scores for different people. Sometimes this overriding criterion may reduce the adequacy of the measurement instrument, for even irrelevant factors may be incorporated in items just to produce variance.

The criterion-referenced item designer is guided by a different principle. His chief purpose is to make sure the item accurately reflects the criterion behavior. Difficult or easy, discriminating or indiscriminate, the item has to represent the class of behaviors delimited by the criterion. This rather fundamental difference in "set" on the part of the criterion-referenced and norm-referenced item constructors can clearly contribute to differences in the resulting items.

Suppose the following item had been prepared by a teacher. Would it be more apt to be suitable for a norm-referenced (N) or a criterion-referenced (C) test? Answer next to Number 7 on the answer sheet.

7.
The multiple choice item with five alternatives is answered correctly by 95 percent of the teacher's class.

You should have circled *C,* for an item which is answered correctly by almost everyone is of little value in "spreading people out." And a norm-referenced test must produce some spread in scores in order to compare different individuals. However, an item which most learners answer correctly, if the item properly reflects the instructional objective, may be quite suitable for criterion-referenced testing.

How about this next item? Is it more likely that it would have been prepared for a norm-referenced or a criterion-referenced test? Answer next to Number 8.

8.
This verbal analogy item was written to measure a person's "native intellectual ability" and, as such, was designed to be answered by only 50 percent of those who attempt it.

You should have circled *N,* since an item which is generally answered by only 50 percent of those attempting it is ideal for purposes of norm-referenced testing.

Once test items are prepared, they are usually tried out and revised in order to improve them. The traditional tool for item revision of norm-referenced test has been "item analysis" and, particularly, the use of discrimination indices. In conducting an item analysis, a norm-referenced measurement specialist tries to locate the following kind of *positively* discriminating item:

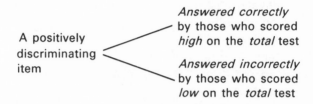

A positively discriminating item

Answered correctly by those who scored *high* on the *total* test

Answered incorrectly by those who scored *low* on the *total* test

Such an item is ideal for purposes of "spreading people out." Items which do not discriminate in this fashion, at least to some extent, are usually modified or eliminated. Nondiscriminating items are generally those which are (a) too easy, (b) too hard, and/or (c) ambiguous. Of course, an item which discriminates in the *wrong* direction must also be altered or discarded. This is what such a *negative discriminator* would look like:

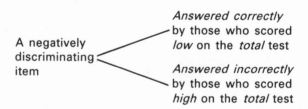

A negatively discriminating item

Answered correctly by those who scored *low* on the *total* test

Answered incorrectly by those who scored *high* on the *total* test

Technically, the numerical index of an item's discriminating efficiency is based on the correlation of the individual item with the total test score, but that will not be treated in detail here.

For criterion-referenced tests, the use of discrimination indices must be modified. An item which doesn't discriminate need not be eliminated. If it reflects an important attribute of the criterion, it should remain in the test. A positively discriminating item is just as respectable in a criterion-referenced test as it is in a norm-referenced test, but is certainly not more so. In fact, if used to assess the effects of instruction, the positively discriminating item may point to areas of instruction in which the program is not succeeding well enough with less able learners. However, negatively discriminating items are treated exactly the same way in a criterion-referenced approach as they are in a norm-referenced approach. When an educational evaluator discovers a negative discriminator in his pool of criterion-referenced items, he is suspicious of it and, after more careful analysis, usually detects flaws in it. Of course, discrimination indices are little more than warning flags; common sense must still be used in weighing the worth of an item identified as a negative discriminator. Now judge whether the following test items would be apt to be more suitable for a norm-referenced or a criterion-referenced test. Answer next to Number 9 by circling the correct letter.

9.

	Percentage answering correctly	Percentage answering incorrectly	Did not attempt to answer
Item #14	97%	2%	1%
Item #26	93%	4%	3%

The correct answer is *C,* because even if an item is answered correctly *by 100 percent* of the learners attempting it, the item may adequately reflect the criterion, hence be suitable.

Items which are answered correctly by almost everyone can contribute little to variant scores, thus are inappropriate for norm-referenced tests.

Turning to reliability, an interesting situation arises. Most educators believe that a test should be highly reliable, that is, it should possess "respectable" reliability coefficients around .90 (the .90 refers to a correlation coefficient reflecting such things as the relationship between scores on two separate administrations of the same test). The more consistently the test measures, the more closely the correlation coefficient approximates 1.0.

NORM-REFERENCED   CRITERION-REFERENCED
RELIABILITY   RELIABILITY

However, correlation coefficients, to be large, must be based on variant scores. And criterion-referenced measures do not necessarily produce variant scores. For norm-referenced measures the classical notions of reliability apply with their usual force, but for criterion-referenced measures they are inappropriate. If, after instruction, *everyone* scores perfectly on a test which accurately reflects the objectives of that instruction, then the test need not be faulted if it produces *no* variability, hence a zero reliability coefficient. If we wish to use the results for evaluating the instructional program, or for placing a learner in the next phase of an instructional sequence, classical reliability coefficients are not necessarily to be sought. Indeed, it is the job of the good teacher to *reduce* criterion performance variability by getting as many pupils as he can to a satisfactory level of competence.

We want our criterion-referenced measures to perform their job with consistency, but the traditional estimates of reliability are simply unsuitable.

Now inspect the results of reliability estimates of the following test and indicate whether it is more apt to be suitable for norm-referenced or for criterion-referenced measurement.

10.

The test	*Reliability estimates*
Designed to measure	Split-half $r = .26$
Punctuation skill	Test-retest $r = .17$

Circle the correct letter by Number 10.

With these low reliability estimates, the test is unsuitable for norm-referenced purposes. If the low reliability estimates are a function of relatively invariant scores, it may be suitable for criterion-referenced purposes. You should have circled *C.*

With norm-referenced measures we are usually interested in making selection decisions regarding individuals. Therefore, the accuracy of those decisions can usually be determined in the context of a predictive validity framework. Were the individuals selected the ones who performed best in some subsequent situation? Correlational approaches allow us to judge the adequacy of such predictions. In other words, we can set up a situation in which we first spread out our individuals through the norm-referenced test, then see if our predictions regarding their performance on some future criterion are accurate.

PREDICTIVE VALIDITY

"REMEMBER, I'LL CHECK UP ON YOU!"

Criterion-referenced measures are validated primarily in terms of the adequacy with which they represent the criterion. A carefully made judgment, based on the test's apparent relevance to the behaviors delimited by the criterion, is the best procedure for validating criterion-referenced measures. Measurement specialists refer to this judgment-based operation as *content* validity. The more precisely instructional objectives can be explicated, therefore, the more accurately we can reach judgments regarding a test's content validity.

Measurement specialists such as Wells Hively and his associates at the University of Minnesota have devised techniques to increase the precision with which content validity can be determined. For each measurably scaled instructional objective an *item form* is written which delimits the form of the test items which may legitimately be used to assess whether the objective has been achieved. In this sense, they have staked out the domain of eligible test items and therefore refer to their approach as *domain-referenced achievement testing.* Although there are a number of practical problems to be worked out in this system, Hively's domain-referenced achievement testing notions appear highly promising.

Would the following approach to validation be more suitable for a norm-referenced or a criterion-referenced approach? Answer next to Number 11 by circling the appropriate letter.

11.
Scores on the measure are correlated with learners' performance three years later.

You should have circled *N.* This is a correlational, not a content validity approach.

Now let's practice deciding whether tests appear more suitable for criterion-referenced or for norm-referenced purposes. In the following few exercises a test will be described. Indicate on your answer sheet, by circling the *C* or *N,* whether you think it is more suitable for one or the other kind of measurement. For the following exercise, answer next to Number 12.

12.
This is a group "intelligence" test designed to identify those elementary school pupils who will do well in secondary school.

The correct answer is *N.*

For the following exercise answer next to Number 13.

13.
This is a highly structured observation sheet used to judge whether preschool children can follow orally presented directions well enough to be enrolled in one type of class rather than another. There are no limitations on enrollment.

The correct answer here is *C.*

Answer next to Number 14 for the following item.

14.
The school social science faculty devised this test to measure whether their new curriculum successfully promoted student ability to describe functions of various branches of the local civic government.

To assess the effectiveness of an instructional sequence, a criterion-referenced test should be used. The correct answer is *C.*

We have seen that there are several differences between norm-referenced and criterion-referenced testing with respect to such operations as test construction, test revision, reliability, and validity. While norm-referenced tests are extremely useful for the purpose for which they are intended, the most appropriate measure of whether or not an instructional objective has been achieved is a *criterion-referenced* test, not a norm-referenced test.

This leads to the final point to be treated in the program: *item sampling*. Both norm-referenced and criterion-referenced measures which are used to make decisions regarding *individuals* require that the same test, or an equivalent form, be used with each individual. However, criterion-referenced tests used for evaluating instructional programs need not be the same for everyone. The concept of item sampling (sometimes referred to as *matrix* sampling) in which different people complete different items, thereby permitting the sampling of more behavior with shorter tests, is highly appropriate for evaluating instructional sequences. Individuals nurtured on the concept of "everybody gets the same items" will often overlook this economic, yet powerful, shortcut.

ITEM SAMPLING

Here's how it works. Suppose you, as teacher, wish to evaluate an eight-week instructional unit you have just completed. You are not concerned for the moment with evaluating individual pupils, but only with evaluating the instructional sequence. You are, in a sense, evaluating yourself rather than your students. Suppose you had 10 objectives and a pool of 10 items for each of the 10 objectives. Rather than giving each child a 100-item test, you could prepare 10 different tests, each with 10 different items. Every test would be composed of items reflecting all ten objectives, but they would be different items. If you have 30 students, you can randomly assign the 10 test forms to the class so that only three pupils complete the same test form. It might look something like this:

Item sampling distribution of tests

Pupil	Test form
John	A
Harry	E
Bill	H
Mary	D
Sue	E
Chris	B
etc.	

In the end, only three pupils would be answering any given item, but each objective would be reflected by *30* different responses. Thus, in evaluating the 10 objectives, in which 10 test items, answered by three pupils per item, yield 30 responses per objective, you would have the following data:

Objective	Percentage correct (of 30 responses to 10 items)
1	83%
2	91%
3	42%
4	78%
etc.	

For evaluating the worth of an instructional sequence it is definitely not necessary to give every learner the same test. For schoolwide evaluation, or in large districts, item sampling can enable more systematic evaluation *while taking far less time from the instructional process.* Hopefully, the concepts treated in this program will become sufficiently accepted by all educational practitioners so that their use will be one of the few stable elements in changing educational practice.

Instructional Supervision: A Criterion-Referenced Strategy

Objectives

This program examines an approach to the evaluation of instruction wherein attention is directed toward the *consequences* of instruction rather than the *means* used during instruction. The program advocates ends-focused instruction as a "criterion-referenced strategy" to be used in the supervisory process. Specifically, at the conclusion of the program the learner should be able to:

1. Describe the two primary functions of an instructional supervisor who uses a criterion-referenced strategy.
2. List four recommended activities to be used by supervisors in carrying out each of these functions.
3. Distinguish between descriptions of supervisory actions and/or decisions which are or are not consistent with a criterion-referenced strategy.

Each year tremendous educational resources, both financial and personnel, are expended on an activity known as instructional supervision. This is not surprising, since the primary mission of instructional supervision is to improve the quality of education. Improved education is a goal worthy of heavy expenditures.

Who are the instructional supervisors? They are all those individuals who devote a significant portion of their professional activities to evaluating and improving the quality of other people's teaching. Instructional supervisors are usually found in all moderately large school districts. In very large districts one can expect to find supervisors in various subject specialties and grade levels. Such individuals are generally responsible for helping a number of teachers in a particular subject or grade level.

Many supervisors are experienced teachers who assist student teachers. These student or practice teachers are typically assigned for a semester or longer to a seasoned teacher under whose direction he engages in limited teaching assignments. The more experienced teacher is usually referred to as the "supervisory teacher," "master teacher," or "training teacher." Whereas these supervising teachers usually take responsibility for only one student teacher at a time, their supervisory goal is essentially similar to that of the district supervisor: they wish to improve the instructional skill of the teacher or teacher-candidate.

There are many other instructional supervisors operating in the nation's education system: numerous college and university supervisors who work with student teachers, leaders of

"HERE'S A GOOD LESSON PLAN I USED IN 1913..."

teaching teams who exercise supervisorial functions with other members of the teaching team, and, in industry and the military, individuals whose responsibility it is to aid those instructors engaged in training operations.

In spite of the many instructional supervisors who are performing their jobs with consummate skill, there are others who could perhaps use an assist or two. This program is designed to provide such assistance. More specifically, it offers a distinctive strategy for approaching instructional supervision. While some supervisors presently employ such strategy, to others it will be new. For those supervisors who see merit in the strategy, it will, hopefully, provide the framework for approaching supervisory responsibilities in a somewhat modified fashion. The approach to instructional supervision to be described in the remainder of the program is known as a *criterion-referenced strategy.*

Let's start with a practical example drawn from the real world of instructional supervision. Examine the following description and decide whether you think it represents a fairly customary type of instructional supervision. If you think this is a somewhat customary form of supervision, circle Yes next to Number 1 on the answer sheet. If not, circle No.

1.

A supervisor arranges with a fourth-grade teacher to visit her class during the language arts period. After viewing the session, the supervisor confers with the teacher and offers suggestions for improved methods of "getting the students involved."

You should probably have answered Yes, for this is a common supervisory practice. Yet—even though this represents the most common form of supervisory activity—*it is indefensible.* It is indefensible because it is focused on the wrong things, namely, what the teacher does. The supervisor should be most attentive not to teacher activity, but to *what happens to the learners* as a consequence of what the teacher does.

A criterion-referenced supervision strategy is based on the assumption that the chief reason a teacher is in the classroom is to promote desirable modifications in learners. If a teacher lectures with the eloquence of Demosthenes, yet his students leave his course basically unchanged, he is an instructional failure. A far less eloquent teacher who brings about worthwhile changes in his learners is an instructional success.

DEMOSTHENES'
PEBBLES
I WEEK'S SUPPLY

Indeed, because the intended change in the learner can be considered the "criterion" by which the instructor can judge the adequacy of his efforts, the instructional supervision scheme described here is known as criterion-referenced supervision. The overriding focus of this approach is on the criterion, that is, the intended change sought in the learner. Operating on the assumption that the teacher's reason for existence in the classroom is to modify his learners, then an important responsibility of the instructional supervisor emerges.

> *Function One:* A criterion-referenced instructional supervisor must help the teacher select more defensible educational objectives.

Since a teacher's educational objectives should reflect his instructional intentions, that is, the intended modifications he hopes to bring about in his learners, his intentions should be as defensible as possible. The instructional supervisor's first job, therefore, is to assist the teacher in making good decisions regarding instructional objectives. The supervisor should aid the teacher in making the best possible curricular choices, for the most critical curriculum decisions are those which involve the selection of objectives.

In fulfilling this first function an instructional supervisor will engage in several activities, usually during face-to-face conferences with the instructor. Here are several steps which can be followed to approach function number one.

> *To select defensible objectives, the supervisor and teacher:*
> 1. Identify any curricular constraints.
> 2. State all objectives operationally.
> 3. Consider alternative objectives.
> 4. Evaluate and decide on each potential objective.

First, the supervisor helps the teacher identify any existing curricular constraints, that is, any state or district regulations which might require the inclusion of certain topics or the promotion of specified goals. Such constraints should be identified early, for they will undoubtedly influence the teacher's selection of objectives.

Second, the supervisor must help the teacher state all objectives in terms of observable learner behaviors. Stating objectives operationally helps to better evaluate the worth of such objectives. When an educator states objectives such as the following: "My students will learn to appreciate the beauty of the English language," few people can quarrel with him—few people know what he means. To judge the adequacy of such an objective we must have it stated in terms of observable learner behaviors. *Then* we can evaluate its worth. The supervisor will find an increasing number of aids such as booklets or filmstrips which can be used to help instructors state their goals operationally.

Third, the supervisor, more experienced in goal-setting, will be able to offer the teacher suggestions regarding goals he might not otherwise have considered. These too, of course, must be stated operationally.

50

Fourth, each potential objective must be individually evaluated. The supervisor and teacher must constantly raise this question: "Is this the most worthwhile behavior change which can be secured from these particular learners?" If the answer is Yes, the objective should be selected; if No, the objective should be deleted.

As indicated, there are other tactics which the criterion-referenced supervisor might employ in fulfilling his first function, but these four steps are helpful. Study these steps briefly.

Next to Number 2 on the answer sheet write, in your own words, four steps to be followed in helping a teacher make more defensible goal selections.

2.
(1) _____
(2) _____
(3) _____
(4) _____

These were the four steps we have been discussing:

> *To select defensible objectives, the supervisor and teacher:*
> 1. Identify any curricular constraints.
> 2. State all objectives operationally.
> 3. Consider alternative objectives.
> 4. Evaluate and decide on each potential objective.

A criterion-referenced instructional supervisor has only two critical responsibilities. His first function is to assist the teacher in making defensible selections of goals. Let's examine function two.

Function Two: A criterion-referenced instructional supervisor assists the teacher in achieving the teacher's instructional objectives.

The second, and in many ways the more challenging, function of a criterion-referenced instructional supervisor is to aid the teacher in attaining his selected objectives.

Although it sounds deceptively simple, anyone who has rigorously approached the task of instructional decision making knows its complexity. But an instructional supervisor who attempts to fulfill this function properly tends to develop a different and far more productive set toward the instructional process. He is *ends-oriented* rather than *means-oriented.*

Consider the following supervisory illustration. Do you think it represents a common occurrence? Circle Yes or No next to Number 3 on the answer sheet.

3.
After viewing Miss Pell, a beginning teacher, for one class period the supervisor offers suggestions for improvement based on the techniques he used with success when he was a classroom teacher.

The correct answer here is Yes, for many supervisors judge the instructional merits of certain classroom practices against the standard of their own "stellar" days in the classroom. But even worse than the fact that a supervisor's memory of his own classroom skill often brightens as the years go by—such supervisors are not attending to the right questions. They are focusing on means, not ends. A criterion-referenced instructional supervisor, after aiding the teacher in the selection of worthwhile goals, always asks the following question:

Have the instructional objectives been achieved?

If the objectives have been achieved without undesirable side effects, then the teacher's instructional procedures *must be considered effective*—even though they might be drastically different from the procedures usually endorsed by the supervisor. *Only* if the instructional objectives have not been achieved does the criterion-referenced supervisor consider the instructional means employed by the teacher. At that point the supervisor is entitled to offer suggestions regarding alternative instructional tactics, for the means currently used by the teacher have not been successful in attaining the intended ends.

You may have noted the brief disclaimer made a moment ago, namely, "if the objectives have been achieved *without undesirable side effects* . . . ." Apply this notion in the following exercise. Should a supervisor be satisfied with this teacher's instructional performance? Answer Yes or No by Number 4.

4.

Mr. Orme attempts to achieve a series of extremely high level objectives in his elective math course. He keeps the class under great pressure to perform well—and this they do on all of his examples. Most students, however, assert they will never take another math class.

No, a supervisor should not be satisfied with Mr. Orme's performance, for although his objectives were apparently achieved, there was an aversive result with respect to student attitude toward the subject. A criterion-referenced supervisor should be attentive to such unanticipated outcomes in deciding whether a teacher's overall performance is satisfactory.

One of the supervisor's best ways to deal with such situations is to aid the teacher identify objectives which describe behavioral indices of student affect, such as interest in the subject matter. One writer has observed that a student should leave an instructional sequence with subject-matter-approaching tendencies equal to or greater than those he had when he began the instructional sequence. The skilled supervisor will be able to help the teacher design measurable objectives which deal with a student's subject-approaching tendencies.

Now let's examine some practice exercises to see if you can decide whether the instructional supervisor is employing a criterion-referenced strategy. For these items, if you think the supervisor *is* using such a strategy, answer Yes. If not, answer No. Answer next to Number 5 for this exercise.

5.

The supervisor notes with some concern that the teacher is using *only* large group activities, yet discovers that the instructional objectives are being achieved well and therefore concludes the instruction is effective.

You should have answered Yes, for the supervisor evaluates the instructional procedures in terms of whether the objectives have been achieved. This is really the heart of a criterion-referenced strategy.

In the next example decide whether the supervisor is employing a criterion-referenced strategy. Answer next to Number 6 by circling the Yes or No.

6.
Miss Carr, a primary supervisor, never observes a teacher's class unless she first has had an opportunity to examine the teacher's goals for that class session. She never comments regarding the class until she examines measures of pupil performance related to the objective.

Miss Carr is employing a criterion-referenced strategy for she apparently bases her evaluation on whether the instructional objectives have been achieved. You should have answered Yes.

Is the supervisor in this next exercise using a criterion-referenced strategy? Answer next to Number 7.

7.
This supervisor observes a teacher's class session and, without determining what the teacher's goals are, offers suggestions for improving the teacher's rapport with the class.

The answer here, of course, is No. This supervisor, like so many other instructional supervisors, is not attentive to the ends achieved by the teacher, but only to the means. And the primary weakness of such a focus is that *there are many ways to achieve an instructional objective.* Perhaps the teacher isn't using one of the supervisor's pet techniques, but the techniques used by the teacher may be working. The supervisor must establish whether the objectives have been achieved *in order* for him to evaluate the adequacy of the instructional techniques.

You will recall that in carrying out his first function, namely, helping the teacher make his objectives more defensible, these four specific steps were recommended.

> *The supervisor and teacher:*
> 1.   Identify any curricular constraints.
> 2.   State all objectives operationally.
> 3.   Consider alternative objectives.
> 4.   Evaluate and decide on each potential objective.

There are also some recommended steps for the supervisor in connection with his second function, that is, helping teachers achieve their objectives. After first having clarified the teacher's objectives,

> *The supervisor:*
> 1.   Determines the teacher's objectives.
> 2.   Secures evidence regarding their achievement.
> 3.   Looks for undesirable side effects.
> 4.   Suggests alternative procedures for unachieved objectives.

First, the supervisor find out what the teacher's objectives are for the segment of instruction under consideration. For example, even though he may have previously worked with the teacher in clarifying the teacher's goals, there is always the question of which particular goals are being sought during the period when the supervisor visits the class.

Second, evidence is gathered regarding whether the objectives have been achieved. Without it no judgments regarding the worth of instructional means should be made. Of course, a teacher doesn't always complete an instructional sequence each day, so a supervisor is well advised to ascertain in advance when data regarding objectives will be available. Third, the supervisor looks for indications that undesirable side effects are present. Is there any evidence, for example, that the learners' interest in the subject has been stifled? Has the intellectual curiosity of the students been dampened? Have they become excessively subservient? Such undesired side effects, if they are clearly present, would suggest the need for a modified approach on the part of the teacher.

Finally, for unachieved objectives the supervisor will suggest alternative instructional procedures which the teacher may wish to implement. If the objectives haven't been achieved, the initial diagnosis is that there is something wrong with the instruction. Different means should be employed. Of course there is always the possibility that the original objectives were set too high for the particular learners at hand. This possibility should be considered, however, only after a number of instructional procedures have been tried and found wanting.

Study these four steps for a moment.

Next to Number 8 on your answer sheet, in your own words, list four recommended steps the criterion-referenced supervisor can use in performing the second of his two functions.

8.

(1) _____

(2) _____

(3) _____

(4) _____

These were the four steps we have been discussing.

> *To aid the teacher achieve objectives, the supervisor:*
> 1. Determines the teacher's objectives.
> 2. Secures evidence regarding their achievement.
> 3. Looks for undesirable side effects.
> 4. Suggests alternative procedures for unachieved objectives.

Let's review for a second. In the spaces provided by Number 9 on the answer sheet, indicate the two primary functions of a criterion-referenced instructional supervisor.

9.
(1) _____
(2) _____

Your answer should have been something like this:

> *The criterion-referenced supervisor's two main functions are to:*
> 1. Help teachers select more defensible objectives.
> 2. Help teachers achieve their objectives.

Of course, there will be other less important responsibilities of any supervisor—but these two are by far the most critical. Note that both functions are focally related to the instructional objective, that is, to the criterion.

We will conclude the program with a series of exercises to see if you can identify when a supervisor is behaving in a fashion consistent with a criterion-referenced strategy. Is the supervisor in this next example using such a strategy? Answer Yes or No next to Number 10.

58

10.

A supervisor has just finished watching an exciting discussion in Miss Teel's social studies class. He observes another teacher's class and, at its conclusion, suggests she use some of the stimulating procedures employed by Miss Teel.

You should have answered No, for this supervisor is attending to means, not ends. The procedures which worked well for Miss Teel may fail abysmally for her colleague. The efficacy of any teaching procedure must be evaluated on the basis of whether it promotes attainment of objectives in the particular situation in which it is used. *If* Miss Teel's colleague is failing to achieve her objectives, *then* the supervisor may suggest that some of Miss Teel's approaches be tried out. But they are *tried out,* much like testing an hypothesis. Their merit is based exclusively on the learner's achievement of the criterion.

How about this next exercise? Is this supervisor employing a criterion-referenced strategy?

11.

Mrs. Blaine always spends the first few visits with any teacher she supervises in a discussion of the teacher's instructional intentions. She tries to clarify the teacher's goals and to encourage the teacher to evaluate each goal.

The correct answer here is Yes. Mrs. Blaine is fulfilling the first function of a criterion-referenced instructional supervisor.

Answer next to Number 12 for the following exercise.

12.
Mr. Colb, a tenth-grade supervising teacher, encourages his student teacher to explicate his objectives in terms of learner behavior. Then, if the objectives are achieved, even if the student teacher employs procedures which Mr. Colb would not use, he praises the student teacher's efforts.

Mr. Colb is behaving most consistently with a criterion-referenced strategy. You should have answered Yes. For the following exercise answer next to Number 13.

13.
Calling upon her years of experience both in the classroom and as a supervisor, Mrs. Carr attends most carefully to the communication style of each teacher she visits. She uses an elaborate check sheet, filled out as the class progresses, to guide her suggestions to the teacher.

You should have answered No here, for Mrs. Carr is too means-oriented to be an effective criterion-referenced supervisor.

For this last exercise, answer by Number 14 on the answer sheet. Is this supervisor using a criterion-referenced strategy?

14.

Although she is satisfied that the teacher she is working with has accomplished his instructional objectives successfully, Miss Bell tries to see if there are any unanticipated negative outcomes of the instructor.

The correct answer here is Yes, for Miss Bell should indeed attend to the possibility of negative side effects. The focus of a criterion-referenced supervisory strategy is on the outcomes produced with learners. In loose terms, the supervisor raises the following two questions with each teacher:

1. What do you want your students to know?
2. After instruction, were your intentions realized?

As indicated earlier, this strategy is based on the assumption that instructors should be *primarily* concerned with modifying their learners. Alternative assumptions appear to be far less tenable.

Constructing
Teaching
Performance
Tests

Objectives

This and the program "Using Teaching Performance Tests" are in a very real sense directed toward an affective goal as much as toward any cognitive outcomes. The desired affective outcome is that the reader will actually use teaching performance in those situations where it can yield useful information. Educators have, through the years, been forced to rely on largely indefensible estimates of teacher effectiveness; the performance test approach offers one useful, but by no means comprehensive, index of a teacher's instructional skill. While a mild effort can be made to assess this affective goal through the use of anonymous self-report questions, it should be clear that the ultimate test of the program's effectiveness will be manifest in the degree to which performance tests are subsequently used by those completing the program.

Specifically, after completing the program the reader will:

1. Be able to describe the rationale underlying the use of teaching performance tests as a measure of teaching skill.
2. Describe in writing the four steps involved in conducting a teaching performance test.
3. Be able to cite in writing the five attributes of an effective teaching performance test (as presented in this program).

Since the beginnings of formal instruction, educators have faced the perplexing problem of how to evaluate a teacher's instructional skill. If we could determine individual teaching skill, we could identify less effective instructors and help them improve. Outstanding teachers could be used as exemplars. The quality of preservice and inservice teacher education programs could be evaluated according to whether they were actually helping teachers improve their skills.

The uses to which a defensible measure of teaching skill can be put are almost limitless. Generally speaking, the two main roles for such a measure would be, first, *instructional improvement* and, second, *skill assessment.* For instructional improvement the measurement procedure would help a teacher get better at instructing learners. For skill assessment the measure would identify weak or strong teachers as an aid to assigning them. For skill assessment such a measure could be used to determine whether inservice or preservice programs were effective.

One would think that this problem would have been solved years ago. But it hasn't yet. Let's examine the three most commonly employed measures of teacher effectiveness to discover why they have not worked.

RATINGS. One of the most frequently used procedures for assessing the teacher's proficiency involves the use of *ratings.* These ratings are usually made by supervisors or administrators, but can also be supplied by the teacher's pupils or colleagues. The rater usually observes the teacher for one or more lessons and then supplies an overall estimate of his instructional competence, or perhaps renders separate ratings of such dimensions as "classroom control," "presentation techniques," etc. But the rater's judgments are often wrong. Most raters have some kind of an idea of how the good teacher should behave in the classroom, but they rarely have evidence to support their views. Typically, administrators recall how they conducted their own courses when they were in the classroom and judge a teacher who fits this image positively. Students sometimes rate a teacher as effective merely because he is entertaining or a lenient grader. In brief, little empirical evidence indicates that ratings of teacher effectiveness are strongly correlated with how much children learn from the teacher. Too many factors limit the usefulness of such ratings as an index of one's teaching skill.

SYSTEMATIC OBSERVATIONS. A second widely used measure of teaching skill is *systematic observation*. A teacher's classroom performance is carefully observed, typically with the aid of some type of check list or observation form, and estimates are provided regarding the frequency with which certain behaviors are displayed, such as the amount of teacher talk, pupil talk, etc. Inherent in most observation approaches is the assumption that certain teacher behaviors are preferable to others. Some advocates of observation approaches actually believe they can identify the *most* effective instructional patterns through the use of such procedures. But the overwhelming verdict of research indicates that no single teaching behavior is invariably associated with learner growth. Different teachers can use markedly different techniques, yet achieve identical results.

While observation procedures can certainly be useful in more adequately describing what goes on in the classroom, reliance on observation procedures tends to focus on instructional *process* to the exclusion of instructional *outcome*. The observer and teacher become so caught up in the intricacies of the procedures used in the classroom that they rarely see what happens to children as a consequence of those procedures.

STANDARDIZED TESTS. The third widely used measure of teaching skill involves the use of *standardized achievement tests* of pupil learning. Quite often, evaluations are made about a teacher, school, or school district on the basis of how pupils perform on commercially distributed achievement measures. A teacher is considered effective if he can increase the number of students performing at or above "grade level." But recent advancements in the field of educational measurement make it apparent that although such tests are well suited for differentiating among individual learners, they are relatively insensitive to the type of learner growth which might appear as a consequence of a particular teacher's efforts. Further, the grossness of measurement indicators yielded by these tests, for example, global "reading comprehension," renders them too imprecise to pick up the sort of instructional impact which a particular teacher might have.

Thus the three most commonly used measures of teaching skill have generally been judged inadequate. Let's check your recollection of what these three approaches are. By Number 1 on the answer sheet, identify with a word or phrase each of these three widely used, albeit unsatisfactory, measures of teaching proficiency.

1.

(1) _____

(2) _____

(3) _____

These, of course, are the three most commonly used indicators of teacher proficiency.

> *Three widely used measures of teacher competence:*
> (1) Ratings
> (2) Systematic observations
> (3) Standardized tests of pupil achievement

But since there are major weaknesses in each, what is the alternative? Fortunately, in the past few years a new technique has been devised for measuring a teacher's instructional skill. While its early use was restricted largely to experimental investigations, the applications in day-to-day educational situations are numerous. The measurement approach involves the use of a *teaching performance test*. This program will show you what a teaching performance test is and how to construct one.

TEACHING PERFORMANCE TESTS: RATIONALE. Use of the teaching performance test is predicated on a central assumption that the chief reason for a teacher's existence is to make beneficial changes in learners, that is, modifications in the learner's knowledge, attitudes, and skills. Now while there are other dimensions on which a teacher may legitimately be evaluated, for instance, how well he gets along with colleagues or parents, teaching performance tests indicate whether the teacher can bring about beneficial changes in learners.

But even though many educators have subscribed to this conception of the teacher's mission, different teachers want to bring about different kinds of changes in their pupils, that is, their *objectives* vary. Even teachers of the same course or grade level will normally have quite different emphases. One U.S. History teacher will stress the Civil War while another will focus on the industrial revolution. When researchers have

tried to use a single learner achievement measure as an indication of teaching skill, they have been unable to take account of these differential emphases.

But what if the objectives were the same? What if we could
see how skillful teachers were at bringing about identical
changes in learners? As you have probably guessed, this is
the essence of the teaching performance test.

*A teaching performance test assesses a teacher's ability to
accomplish prespecified changes in learners, using whatever
instructional procedures the teacher wishes.*

By keeping the objectives constant, and allowing the teacher
to use whatever instructional tactics he thinks best to achieve
those objectives, we can compare teachers with respect to
their ability to promote the pupil's attainment of prespecified
instructional objectives. Here are the four major steps in how
a teaching performance test is used.

STEP 1. The teacher is given one or more explicit instructional objectives and a sample of the measurement proce-

dure to assess each objective, plus any necessary background information related to the objectives.

STEP 2. The teacher is given sufficient time to plan a lesson to accomplish the objectives.

STEP 3. The teacher then instructs a group of learners, previously identified as being unable to accomplish the given objectives, in an effort to have the learners achieve those objectives.

STEP 4. At the conclusion of the lesson the learners are measured with respect to their ability to accomplish the objectives, their performance serving as an estimate of the teacher's instructional skills.

Before turning to the specific procedures used to develop such performance tests, let's briefly look at each of these four steps in a bit more detail.

> *Step 1.* The teacher is given the objective(s) and necessary background information.

First, the teacher must be given an extremely clear statement of what the objective is for the lesson. Such an objective must be stated in terms of measurable learner performance which will be assessed after the lesson. A sample item from the posttest will also further clarify the nature of the objective. There must be no uncertainty in the teacher's mind regarding the instructional task at hand.

The background information might be nothing more than a one or two page handout giving facts or other details which an instructor might need. For example, if the objective deals with an obscure segment of Egyptian history, the teacher might be given a brief written account of this historical period.

Step 2. The teacher plans the lesson.

The second step involves the teacher's planning of a lesson designed to achieve the objectives which have been given. Usually the time available for the lesson itself will be brief, merely for economy of utilization. For example, teaching performance tests have been used successfully for instructional periods as short as ten minutes or as long as two weeks. Performance tests involving a 30-minute lesson have proven adequate in detecting differences among teachers. For a 15-minute lesson, for example, it might be sufficient to allow the teacher several hours, or a full day to plan the lesson. In planning the lesson the teacher is encouraged to use instructional procedures that seem most suitable to him. Any pedagogical preferences are clearly the teacher's in this situation.

Step 3. The teacher conducts the lesson.

Third, the teacher next conducts the lesson with pupils who have been identified as instructionally naive, that is, unable to accomplish the objectives under consideration. If the objectives deal with a topic with which the learners might be familiar, they will have to be pretested to make sure the intended behavior is not already within their repertoires. If the objectives are based on an esoteric topic, for example, a newly constructed verbal code, then pretesting is probably not necessary. The teacher may or may not be familiar with the learners. Sometimes a whole class of pupils will be involved, sometimes only a handful.

Step 4. The learners are posttested.

At the close of the lesson the learners are measured with respect to the objectives. If the objective involved teaching the learners a multiplication skill involving pairs of triple digit numbers, then the pupils would be given a posttest consisting of triple digit multiplication problems. This posttest would *not* have been seen previously by the teacher, although its essential nature could have been inferred from the objectives. The teacher's ability to bring about prespecified behavior changes in learners is, of course, reflected by the pupils' performance on the posttest. A rating of the learners' interest in the lesson can also be secured at this time.

Recapitulating, these then are the four steps in conducting a teaching performance test. Study them briefly, for in a moment you will be asked to list them.

> (1) The teacher is given the objective and any necessary background information.
> (2) The teacher plans the lesson.
> (3) The teacher conducts the lesson.
> (4) The learners are posttested.

Now without referring to the text, see if you can recall these four steps by listing them, in your own words, beside Number 2 on your answer sheet.

2.

(1) _____

(2) _____

(3) _____

(4) _____

Check your answer to see if you have identified the four steps correctly.

The actual uses of teaching performance tests for the teacher's own instructional improvement as well as in teaching skill assessment are described in the next program. Let's turn our attention to how such performance tests are actually constructed.

There are at least five attributes which an effective teaching performance test should possess. We'll first examine each of these five elements briefly, then treat all of them in more detail.

First, the instructional objective or objectives for the test must be readily measurable; they must be stated in terms of learner behavior which can be assessed after the teacher's lesson. At the same time the objective or objectives must be achievable in the time designated for the lesson. For example, if a 20-minute performance test were being constructed, then the objective should not cover the rise of the Roman Empire, much less its fall. Attainability of the objective depends, of course, on the learners to be taught. It is particularly important that the approximate age level and general characteristics of the intended learners be clearly specified. For instance, is the performance test to be used with junior high school youngsters of average ability, or only with bright six-to eight-year-olds?

Second, the objective or objectives for the test should be based on a topic or skill to which the intended learners have had little or no previous exposure. Often this will mean that the test deals with novel subject matter. Care should be taken, however, that the content is not so esoteric that the learner will view it as absurd, thereby reducing the likelihood that he will put forth his best effort.

Third, the teacher will need to be given any background information needed to achieve the objective. To be practical, the information should not be so extensive that it will take up too much of the teacher's time. For example, with a short performance test, a handout of three or four pages might suffice.

Fourth, the scheme to measure the degree to which the learners have achieved the objective must be completely consonant with the objective originally given the teacher. There should not be trickery in a well-constructed teaching performance test. In addition, the measurement procedures should be relatively straightforward to administer, and should not take too much of the learner's time.

Finally, when used by numerous teachers with the intended

learners, the test must be able to detect differences in teacher ability to achieve the test's objectives. In other words, for the time period for which it is designed the test cannot be so easy that all teachers achieve the objectives with all learners, nor so hard that no teachers achieve the objectives with any learners. There should be a range of performance displayed by teachers who complete the test. For the test to be useful in either skill assessment or instructional improvement, it must be able to pick up some of the variation in instructional effectiveness which is obviously present in real life.

SOPHISTICATED MEASUREMENT

Let's examine each of these five attributes in more detail and decide whether hypothetical performance tests possess the attributes.

> 1. Objectives must be measurable and attainable in the time available.

In order to communicate to the teacher precisely what the instructional task is, the objective for the performance test must be stated in unambiguous terms. The objective should describe the measurable learner behavior that the teacher will try to produce as a consequence of his instruction. Educators often refer to such statements of objectives as behavioral or performance objectives. (There are now many reference books and other instructional aids available on this way of stating objectives.) If the teaching performance test has more than one objective, as might be the case for longer performance tests, all objectives should be measurable. A sample test item for each objective from the posttest can give the teacher an even clearer conception of what is to be taught.

Which of the following objectives is stated properly for a teaching performance test? Circle the letter of the properly stated objective by Number 3 on your response sheet.

3.
A.   Using the International Morse Code the learner will be able to transmit three previously unencountered one-sentence messages on the telegraph key so that an experienced operator can understand them.
B.   Students will be able to display markedly increased understanding of the historical antecedents of the War of 1812.

Of these two objectives, the first is clearer by far. For clarity's sake, the person constructing the performance test should also add one or more sample test items; in the case of objective A, these items would be sample one-sentence messages which might be employed after instruction to measure the objective.

While the performance test constructor must be sure to state the objectives in measurable form, he should also make sure that the objective is reasonably achievable in the available time. For example, which of these topics would probably be suitable for a 30-minute performance test? Answer by Number 4 on the response sheet. More than one answer may be correct.

4.
A. Historical antecedents of fifteen services provided by the United Nations.
B. The membership of the U.S. Cabinet.
C. Three key differences between Doric and Corinthian architecture.
D. History of African independence movements from 1900 to the present.

Topics B and C appear sufficiently restrictive to be a reasonably attainable objective for a 30-minute performance test. The other two topics appear to be too broad. Of course, the crucial element is the actual objective to be accomplished. But in devising a teaching performance test it is probably best to start with a topic or skill that is fairly modest in its scope.

Working with both these considerations, that is, measurability and time suitability, which one of the following objectives would probably be best for a one-hour performance test? Answer by Number 5.

5.
A. The learner will be able to place kick successfully 8 out of 10 field goals from 30 yards away on a muddy football field.
B. Learners will feel more positively regarding the plight of the American Eskimo.
C. Pupils can accurately play a simple melody on a mouth harp given a new musical score involving 5–10 notes.

Of these three objectives, choice C is the best. While objective A is stated measurably, it unquestionably represents a skill not readily transmitted in one hour. Objective B is not stated measurably. Objective C could probably be further clarified, particularly regarding the determination that the learner is playing "accurately," but it is clearly the best of the three.

> 2. Objective(s) should be unfamiliar to learner, but not seem absurd.

The second attribute of an effective teaching performance test requires the intended learner to be sufficiently unfamiliar with the topic to display learning as a consequence of the teacher's instruction. If a conventional topic is selected, such as reading or mathematics, then the task is to locate learners who have not already achieved the objective to be taught. As this requires extra administrative effort, teaching performance tests are often constructed with novel subject matter. For example, rather than use a standard objective in reading, Professor John McNeil, one of the early advocates of the performance test strategy, devised new codes and code-breaking skills to be taught which were analogous to those encountered by the nonreader as he learns to read.

But while the topic for the performance test is often novel, it should not be patently silly. Which one of these topics would seem to be both unfamiliar yet potentially important to the learner? Circle the best answer by Number 6.

6.
A. How to punctuate sentences.
B. Basic elements of the Amharic language of Ethiopia.
C. Potentially dangerous ingredients in soft drinks.
D. Memorizing nonsense syllables.

Choice C is preferable here, for it deals with a topic which is probably unfamiliar to most learners but which they would deem worthwhile. Topic A is one with which many learners are already familiar. Topic B is novel, but probably too remote for most learners. Topic D would obviously be hard to defend as relevant to just about anything. Let's look at attribute three again.

> 3. Background information for the teacher should be adequate but brief.

Because the objective for the performance test may deal with an unfamiliar topic, the teacher must be given requisite information so that a lesson can be planned to accomplish the objective. Yet, because these performance tests must be practical to be useful, the teacher should not be burdened with too much background reading. For short duration performance tests, a few pages of reading material would probably be the maximum. For longer performance tests, of course, the teacher might be given more extensive materials.

"TO PREPARE FOR THIS 2 HR. PERFORMANCE TEST YOU HAVE EXACTLY 39 SECONDS!"

Do you suppose the teacher in the following example would approach her teaching performance test with a positive attitude? Answer Yes or No next to Number 7.

7.
Prior to preparing her lesson for a half-hour teaching performance test, Miss Malcomb is directed to read a 120-page technical monograph on the mating habits of the heterosexual pollywog.

Undoubtedly Miss Malcomb would not be too positive regarding her performance test, for the reading expenditure she is asked to make is not warranted by the half-hour teaching performance test. Keep the background information as brief as possible, while making sure it is sufficient for the objective under consideration.

> 4.   The posttest should be congruent with the objectives and easy to administer.

The fourth attribute of an effective performance test concerns the measurement procedures which are used after instruction to discern whether the objective has been achieved. For one thing, the posttest must be completely congruent with the objective the teacher is trying to achieve. The person designing the teaching performance test should call in one or more colleagues to judge whether the posttest is consistent with the objective. And posttest refers here to any type of measurement device, not merely a paper and pencil test. While the teacher is not given the actual items used to posttest the learners, the nature of those items should be readily inferable from the objective and sample item provided prior to instruction.

Which, for example, of the items following this objective would be congruent with the objective. Choose the best test item and answer by Number 8 on the response sheet.

8.
Objective: The learner will be able to multiply correctly any pair of double-digit numbers.

Items: A. 41
       X<u>37</u>
       B. What is the product of 27 and 9?
       C. What does it mean to "carry" numbers when multiplying?

Clearly, test item A is the appropriate item.

A second consideration in devising a good posttest is its easy administration. Usually, the performance test will deal with a cognitive objective and related test items. Try to construct at least five to ten test items so that even a few learners can complete a sufficiently large number of items to adequately represent whether the objective has really been achieved. (Incidentally, using multiples of five items makes it simple to calculate percentages.)

> 5. The test must be able to discriminate among teachers.

A final and particularly important attribute of a well-constructed teaching performance test is that it can pick up differences among teachers in their instructional skill. The objective should be sufficiently difficult to accomplish with the intended learners so that some, but not all, teachers can accomplish it. Without trying it out, of course, there is no way to be certain that a newly devised performance test will discriminate among teachers. But the person building a performance test at least can attempt to avoid the weaknesses of a test that is so hard that few teachers can achieve the objective or so easy that almost all teachers can. The test should be field tested with a number of teachers and appropriate learners. The results of such field tests should dictate whether revisions are required.

For example, suppose that three different versions of a 15-minute performance test had been prepared and field tested, each with five teachers instructing groups of six learners. For each version of the performance test a ten-item examination serves as the posttest. With the following field test results representing the average number right per pupil on the ten-item test, which version appears most suitable? Answer by Number 9

9.

Version A		Version B		Version C	
Teacher	#Right	Teacher	#Right	Teacher	#Right
1	3	1	3	1	10
2	6	2	2	2	9
3	5	3	1	3	8
4	10	4	2	4	10
5	9	5	2	5	10

Since Version A produces the most variability, it is the most suitable. Version B appears to be too difficult, and Version C too easy.

For a performance test which, on the basis of a field trial, does not discriminate, several things can be done. The diffi-

culty level of the objective can be altered. The difficulty of the posttest items can also be modified, for even though we might like our objective to be written with sufficient specificity that only a single difficulty level test item could be written to measure it, there is usually some slack in the difficulty level with which test items might be written to measure even precise objectives. Then, too, the time level permitted for the performance test can also be altered. For example, less time can be allowed to accomplish easy objectives. In addition, the kinds of learners with whom the test is to be used can be changed—for instance, older or younger children can be employed.

For a moment, review the five attributes of an effective teaching performance test.

1. The objective must be measurable and attainable in the time available.
2. The objective should be unfamiliar to the learner but not absurd.
3. Background information for the teacher should be adequate but brief.
4. The posttest should be congruent with the objective and easy to administer.
5. The test must be able to discriminate among teachers.

Now, without referring to the text, in your own words describe each of these five attributes on your answer sheet next to Number 10.

10.
(1) _____
(2) _____
(3) _____
(4) _____
(5) _____

Check your answers to see if you included the five attributes we have been discussing.

For practice see if you can detect weaknesses in teacher performance tests, that is, performance tests which do not incorporate these attributes. What, if anything, is clearly wrong with the following performance test? There may, incidentally, be more than one defect. Answer by Number 11 in the spaces provided.

11.
This 30-minute performance test, to be used with junior high school youngsters, has the following objective: "Learners will be able to display increased knowledge of U.S. History." The teacher is asked to complete a textbook (209 pages) prior to planning the lesson.

The most obvious weaknesses in this test are the nonmeasurability of the objective and the excessive reading requirement asked of the teacher. The topic will also probably be familiar to the learners. Incidentally, many teachers err in building their first performance tests by making their objective totally dependent for interpretability on the posttest. That is, they state objectives such as "The learner will get at least 90 percent of the posttest items correct." Yet, since the teacher does not have access to the posttest, such objectives obviously do not communicate well. For a final exercise, see if there are any clear weaknesses in the following performance test. Answer by Number 12.

12.
The topic for this 20-minute performance test is attitudinal. The teacher is to increase the students' frustration tolerance so that they will be able to cope more effectively with their daily problems. In a field trial the anonymous questionnaires used to measure the objective's attainment reveal little progress for most learners.

One significant defect in the performance test is the unrealistic objective for a 20-minute teaching period. Clearly, bringing about the intended kind of affective change would take more than 20 minutes. Thus, the test does not discriminate among teachers. A more modest objective should have been chosen.

This program has described the underlying rationale and given suggestions for constructing teaching performance tests. There are innumerable situations in which the astute educator can employ such measures. If commercially available teaching performance tests suit a local need, they should be employed.[1] If additional performance tests are constructed, this program will hopefully be of some assistance.

[1]Such tests are distributed by *Instructional Appraisal Services,* Box 24821, Los Angeles, California 90024.

Using
Teaching
Performance
Tests

Objectives

As with the preceding program, this program is designed both to promote specific cognitive skills as well as dispose the reader to use teaching performance tests in one or both of the roles described in the program.

Specifically, after completing the program the reader will:

1. Be able to describe the two chief roles of teaching performance tests.
2. For given situations, be able to indicate correctly whether teaching performance tests should be used chiefly for instructional improvement or for skill assessment.
3. Designate whether given procedures associated with the use of teaching performance tests are recommended for (a) instructional improvement, (b) skill assessment, or (c) both.
4. Given fictitious or real descriptions of educators employing teaching performance tests, be able to identify any errors in the use of the tests.

A teaching performance test provides an opportunity for a teacher to assess his instructional effectiveness by attempting to accomplish prespecified instructional objectives in a relatively short time period. Although a description of the rationale and construction procedures for such tests was presented in the program "Constructing Teaching Performance Tests," a brief explanation of the teaching performance test approach is in order.

First, a teacher is given one or more highly explicit instructional objectives, usually accompanied by a sample test item, then allowed sufficient time to plan a lesson so that a group of learners can achieve the objective. Customarily, the topic for the objective will be novel, thereby reducing prior learner familiarity with the objective. The teacher is also given any necessary background information regarding the topic and a general description of the kinds of learners to be taught. After the teacher carries out the lesson, a posttest is administered to the learners. The posttest is not previously available to the teacher, but its form is readily inferable from the explicit objective which the teacher is attempting to accomplish. The learners' ability to achieve the preset objective serves as a measure of the teacher's instructional skill. While other dimensions undoubtedly should be considered in judging the quality of a teacher, the ability to bring about intended improvements in learners is certainly one important factor. This program will describe two different uses for teaching performance tests and will offer recommended procedures for each of these uses.

The two chief roles for a teaching performance test are *instructional improvement* and *skill assessment.* When a performance test is used for *instructional improvement,* the focus of the activity is on increasing the teacher's skill in promoting learner attainment of prespecified goals. No attempt is made to classify the teacher as weak or strong; the sole purpose of using the performance test is to help the teacher get better at achieving objectives. Teaching performance tests are used for *skill assessment* to find out which teachers are superior

and which are inferior with respect to this particular compe-
tency, that is, the ability to accomplish prespecified instructional objectives. It must be reemphasized that the skill being
assessed is only *instructional* skill and there are clearly other
attributes on which a teacher should be evaluated. Let's see,
however, if you can distinguish between situations which
seem to call for these two different uses of teaching performance tests. Later on we'll examine some variations in the
use of performance tests for these two purposes.

In the following situation should a performance test be employed for instructional improvement or for skill assessment?
Answer by Number 1 on your answer sheet.

1.
A group of elementary school teachers is dissatisfied with their
pupils' performance in basic arithmetic. They decide to devote the
second half of the school year to an inservice program which will
help all the teachers do a better job.

This is a fairly obvious instance where performance tests should be used for instructional improvement rather than for skill assessment. An inservice improvement program could be organized around short term performance tests in mathematics. Each week after school one of the teachers could take a turn at instructing a small group of learners, perhaps for only 15–20 minutes, while his colleagues looked on. Based on the results of the posttest, the group could exchange views regarding how the lesson could have been improved and what features of the lesson appeared to be particularly effective. In this type of situation teaching becomes *public* rather than *private,* and the results of analyses based on post-instruction learner performance should prove beneficial both to the teacher carrying out the performance test and to the observers. Clearly, the atmosphere of the postperformance test discussions should be improvement-focused and *absolutely nonpunitive* in nature.

Here is another situation often faced by educators. Should performance tests be used here for instructional improvement or for skill assessment? Answer by Number 2.

2.
A high school principal wishes to institute a differentiated staffing plan whereby certain teachers instruct large groups of pupils and others work with smaller groups. He wants to find out which teachers in his present faculty are best suited for each role.

To find the best of anything implies comparisons. When comparisons among teachers are required, performance tests must be used for skill assessment. In this instance, performance tests could be set up using both large and small groups of learners so that the relative instructional skill of teachers in both situations could be appraised. Subsequent staffing assignments could be made with such results playing at least a partial role in the decision.

Is the instructional improvement or skill assessment role involved here? Circle your answer by Number 3.

3.

A college teacher education program is requested to supply the school's placement office with information regarding the relative effectiveness of each credential candidate. School hiring officials are demanding this information in view of the excessive number of applicants for each teaching position.

The school placement office clearly needs skill assessment information. The teacher education program could institute an end-of-program assessment scheme in which each credential candidate could display his instructional skill in several performance test situations. Such results could be included in each candidate's professional folder along with other pertinent data.

How about this next situation? Should performance tests be used for instructional improvement or skill assessment? Circle the correct answer next to Number 4 on your answer sheet.

4.

Mrs. Finch has been teaching for four years and feels she has "gone stale" in the classroom. She confides to her husband that she can't even tell any more whether she's doing a good or bad teaching job.

This is a sticky choice. The best answer is probably instructional improvement, for Mrs. Finch really needs to acquire skills to get better at her job. More specifically, she needs to know when she's doing a good or bad job and this obviously implies the necessity to determine her skill. Even when used for instructional improvement, there is an element of skill assessment involved with teaching performance tests, for one can discern the *degree* to which objectives have been achieved. But if the focus is on the teacher's getting better, as it is here, rather than on making a placement or tenure decision, then the instructional improvement role is principally involved.

Let's review. In the spaces by Number 5 on your answer sheet, briefly describe the two chief roles of teaching performance tests that we have been discussing.

5.
(1) _____
(2) _____

In your own words you should have indicated that the instructional improvement role is designed to make the teacher a more effective accomplisher of prespecified objectives, while the skill assessment role is designed to measure a teacher's current skill in achieving such objectives (and usually contrasts that skill with the skills of other).

Let's turn now to an examination of specific ways in which teaching performance tests are used for these two programs. While the uses of performance tests definitely differ for skill assessment and for instructional improvement, there are also recommended procedures for using performance tests in either situation. We'll examine the five common procedures first, since they should be followed when using teaching performance tests for both skill assessment and for instructional improvement.

For instructional improvement and skill assessment:
1. Allow sufficient planning time for the teacher.

In order for a teaching performance test to yield a meaningful estimate of how well an instructor can accomplish preset instructional goals, the instructor must be allowed a reasonable time to plan an instructional sequence. Indeed, the very conception of the teaching performance test rests on the premise that a teacher should display his best effort to bring about the specified behavior changes in the learners. Insufficient planning time would preclude this possibility.

What is the least amount of planning time which should be available, particularly for short term performance tests? Well, for a very brief performance test with a 10 to 15 minutes lesson limit, the teacher should probably be given at least one hour to plan the lesson (not counting the time necessary to read through any background material). If a brief pamphlet must first be read, then a planning hour should be provided beyond the time needed to read the pamphlet. If it is convenient, of course, more planning time should be permitted. The teacher is not required to use all of the planning time and, in fact, may use only a small portion of it. Yet, allowing ample planning time avoids the danger that the teacher will reject the performance test approach merely because he was "too rushed."

For instructional improvement and skill assessment:
2. Use naive but teachable learners.

A second recommended procedure concerns the learners to be employed during the lesson. The learners to be used must not have already achieved the objectives to be taught, but must have a reasonable chance of doing so. In other words, a group of appropriate learners must be located to whom the objective or objectives of the performance test will, at the outset, be unfamiliar but reasonably attainable. It may be necessary to try out the given performance test on a few persons from the pool of learners under consideration to be certain that the larger group will be suitable for that particular performance test.

It would obviously be inappropriate to ask a teacher to promote given behavior changes in learners when, in fact, the learners already possessed that behavior. Similarly, it would be grossly misleading to assign a group of learners to a teacher when, for lack of aptitude or other reasons, the objectives to be taught were simply unachievable in the available instructional time. Obviously, learners for performance tests should be selected with great care.

> *For instructional improvement and skill assessment:*
> 3.   Use small or large groups of learners.

A third recommended procedure for using performance tests concerns the numbers of learners to be used. Either very small groups of learners, as few as three or four per group, or much larger, normal classroom groups can be utilized satisfactorily. The major consideration is convenience. If it is administratively more simple to use extant class groups, rather than to assemble small groups, then by all means employ the larger groups. If it is easier to use small groups, then opt for fewer learners. Since it is not necessary for the teacher to be familiar with the learners, considerable flexibility is available regarding learner group size.

> *For instructional improvement and skill assessment:*
> 4.   Item sampling posttests may be used.

A fourth consideration involves the administration of the post-test after the lesson has been completed. Since the actual posttest has not been seen by the teacher until this point, it is often administered to the learners by someone other than the teacher. Because we are anxious to make teaching procedure tests easy to use, we can employ a time-saving short cut with larger learner groups. Imagine you have an eight-item posttest and a group of 12 learners. Rather than giving all eight items to each learner, you could randomly split the 12 learners into two groups of six learners each and give four items to each group. You'll still have six responses to each of the eight test items and, since it is the *average* performance of the learner group that is of interest, this information would be quite sufficient.

"FOR TODAY'S POSTTEST YOU EACH WILL RECEIVE 1/3 OF A TEST ITEM."

ITEM SAMPLING

With larger groups you can employ only a single item per learner and still attain a perfectly defensible estimate of how well the total group has performed. This technique of having different learners complete less than the total test is referred to as *item sampling.* The procedure was briefly described in a previous program, "Modern Measurement Methods."

While measurement specialists are beginning to study item sampling intensively—we may expect explicit guidelines in the future regarding the minimum number of items per learner which can provide us with a legitimate group estimate—no satisfactory guidelines of this type exist at this moment. Thus, the degree to which item sampling should be employed will depend on the importance of the use to which the performance test is being put. For casual instructional improvement situations we might use item sampling with only a handful of learners. When the stakes are higher, more items per learner should be used.

> *For instructional improvement and skill assessment:*
> 5.   Routinely assess learner affect.

The fifth recommended procedure dictates that the learner's affective response to the instructional situation should always be assessed. Simple little anonymous response sheets which ask one or more questions such as "Did you find the topic of the lesson interesting?" or "Did you enjoy the lesson?" should be distributed and collected after the posttest. In real teaching situations many instructors bring about cognitive achievement at the expense of positive learner affect toward the subject matter. There are numerous examples of teachers who, for instance, teach the students to learn mathematics but also to hate it. An effective teacher should be able to accomplish objectives while not promoting aversive affective side effects. Learner affective response should always be appraised as one studies the learner's regular posttest results.

Reviewing, then, we have examined five recommended procedures to be employed irrespective of whether the teaching performance test is being used for instructional improvement or skill assessment. Study them for a moment. Shortly, you will be asked to reproduce them in your own words.

1. Allow sufficient planning time for the teacher.
2. Use naive but teachable learners.
3. Use small or large groups of learners.
4. Item sampling posttests may be used.
5. Routinely assess learner affect.

Now, next to Number 6 on the response sheet, see if you can cite each of these five recommended practices without referring to the text. Any order is acceptable.

6.
(1) _____
(2) _____
(3) _____
(4) _____
(5) _____

Check the accuracy of your answers by referring to the above list.

But whereas these five procedures should be used whenever teaching performance tests are employed, two distinctive procedures should be followed when performance tests are used for *instructional improvement.* First, to really derive the maximum benefit from using performance tests to improve instruction, careful analysis of the instruction must be undertaken.

> *For instructional improvement:*
> 1. Clinical observers should conduct instructional analyses based on learner performance.

Ideally, colleagues of the teacher completing the performance test should observe the instruction, preferably after having access to any written instructional plans the teacher has prepared. After the posttest has been given and achievement of the objective can be determined, then a clinical analysis of the instruction can take place involving the teacher and the observers. Such analyses must stem from considerations of what happened to the pupils as a consequence of instruction. Otherwise, the analysis session will turn into a typical process-focused discussion in which one person's estimate of good teaching technique is argued against another's. If the objectives have been achieved, student affect is positive, and no unanticipated negative side effects are present, then *by definition* the instructional procedures were effective. The clinical analysis should isolate those procedures which particularly seemed to contribute to the good results.

On the other hand, if the objectives were not achieved or if student affect was negative, then suggestions for modification in the instructional sequence should be considered. At this point suggestions offered for different teaching tactics are essentially hypotheses to be tested via subsequent performance tests. This leads to the second procedure to be followed when using performance tests for instructional improvement.

For instructional improvement:
2.   Provide opportunities for replanning and reteaching unsuccessful lessons.

If a teacher is unable to accomplish the preset objectives of a performance test, or if the resulting learner affect is negative, the teacher should definitely have a chance to try out a revised instructional strategy. This step, perhaps more than any other, is the key to using a teaching performance test for instructional improvement. After an analysis of an ineffective instructional sequence, alternative instructional tactics should be formulated and tried out with a new group of learners. Once more the merits of these new procedures should be judged in terms of the results displayed by learners after the lesson. If the new instructional procedures fail, then others should be devised and tried out.

1.   Performance-based clinical analysis
2.   Reteaching opportunities

The above two ingredients, therefore, are requisite when using teaching performance tests to improve instruction.

Now we'll give you some practice in deciding whether, for purposes of instructional improvement, some fictitious instructors are properly using teaching performance tests. Next to Number 7 on your answer sheet indicate whether this teacher was following recommended procedures.

7.

By pairing with another teacher, Mrs. Lee takes turns being teacher or observer as she uses 30-minute performance tests for two weeks during her preparation period. She and her colleague criticize each other, then revise ineffective lessons and teach them again.

Mrs. Lee and her associate are using performance tests for instructional improvement quite properly. You should have answered Yes. Here is a more difficult exercise. See if you think this instructor is, in general, using teaching performance tests properly for purposes of instructional improvement. Answer next to Number 8.

8.
Mr. Poe has been unable to find someone to observe him as he completes a series of 10-minute performance tests. Nevertheless, after each lesson is completed, he has students administer their own posttests, then tries to think through his lesson on the basis of the posttest results. He tries to avoid apparently weak procedures in future lessons.

Although Mr. Poe does not have the benefit of another person to aid him in his clinical analyses, he appears to be doing the best he can under the circumstances. You should have answered Yes. Undoubtedly, several observers would make the clinical analysis sessions far more productive. In their absence, however, Mr. Poe might try to secure some data regarding how well other teachers had been able to do with the performance tests he was using, thereby supplying himself with at least a rough comparative standard.

Let's now turn to the tricky question of how to use teaching performance tests for *skill assessment.* Four recommended procedures, if followed properly, can permit the use of teaching performance tests and can make reasonably justifiable estimates regarding the relative instructional skill of different teachers. Remember that the proficiency a teacher displays on a teaching performance test is only a single criterion, although an important one, by which a teacher should be evaluated.

Muirhead Library
Michigan Christian College
Rochester, Michigan

Before turning specifically to the four recommended procedures, a word or two regarding the problem of instructional
skill assessment is in order. When we evaluate someone's
teaching skill we are typically making a *comparative* judgment. Is Teacher *A* better than Teacher *B?* Is Teacher *B* better
now than he was *before?* How many teachers can reach a
given level of competence on certain performance tests?
Such questions accurately suggest that teaching skill assessment generally involves *comparing* the effectiveness with
which different teachers can accomplish the objectives stipu-
lated in a performance test. Sometimes the comparisons will
need to be made in only very general terms, for instance:
"After a one-year inservice skill building program, 49 percent
of the district teachers were able to exceed their previous
performance on comparable teaching performance tests." In
other situations more precise comparisons will be required.
For example, if only one physics teacher within a high school
faculty is to be assigned to an important television teaching
position, then obviously we must try to identify, by comparison, the best physics teacher. Similarly, even when a teacher
contrasts his current versus his past teaching skill, he is definitely engaged in comparison. Thus, as we deal with the recommended procedures for skill assessment, do not be
surprised that they generally stem from the necessity to engage in comparative appraisals.

> *For skill assessment:*
> 1. All relevant conditions should be comparable for
> each teacher.

The first recommended procedure concerns the necessity to
provide equal success opportunities for all teachers. No
teacher should be initially disadvantaged because other
teachers have had the benefit of, for example, more preparation time or greater familiarity with the topic involved in the
performance test. Thus, we would want to be particularly
careful not to use performance tests which treated objectives
that were well known to only some, but not all, of the partic-

ipating teachers. Suppose a performance test dealt with an advanced topic in mathematics. Certainly, if only some participating teachers were familiar with advanced mathematics, then the other teachers would be at a disadvantage. It is for this reason that performance tasks are often constructed

"YOUR PERFORMANCE TEST IS BASED ON MY DAUGHTER-IN-LAW'S DIARY."

around novel subject matter, for not only will such subject matter be unfamiliar to students, but to teachers as well. The essence of this recommended procedure is to remove obvious sources of inequity in the conditions associated with teachers' use of performance tests for skill assessment.

For skill assessment:
2.   Assign learners to teachers randomly.

The second recommended procedure for skill assessment requires that learners be assigned to teachers randomly, thereby reducing the likelihood that a teacher will be advantaged or disadvantaged by getting a particularly bright or particularly dull group of learners. Rather than using intact classes, assign learners randomly from a well-defined pool of learners. Preferably this learner pool will have no markedly deviant (exceptionally weak or strong) learners within it. Randomized assignment, perhaps through the use of a table of random numbers, is a powerful way of minimizing initial ability differences in the learner groups assigned to a teacher. There is, of course, the possibility that even with randomization of assignment a teacher might be forced to work with an abstract group of learners. This leads to the third recommended procedure.

For skill assessment:
3. More than one performance test should be completed by each teacher.

Because of the possibility of an *atypical* result on a single performance test, the teacher must have more than one opportunity to display his skill. Would a school administrator have more confidence in ascribing a positive recommendation to a teacher who had performed well on a single teaching performance test or to a teacher who had done well on four of five different performance tests? Clearly, a more representative estimate of one's teaching skill can be secured if more than one performance test is used. At the absolute minimum, two performance tests should be employed.

For skill assessment:
4. Preserve test security.

Because in some instances important decisions will be made on the basis of performance tests used for skill assessment, it is imperative that participating teachers not have access to the tests prior to their use. Therefore, if commercial versions of performance tests are employed, those using the tests either must be certain that the participating teachers have not had prior access to the tests or, more likely, will have to construct new performance tests for local skill assessment use. It is crucial that locally developed performance tests be field tested carefully to make sure they are suitable. Once a pool of local tests is devised, of course, its security should be carefully preserved.

Reviewing, then, we have examined these four recommended procedures when using performance tests for skill assessment.

> *For skill assessment:*
> 1. All relevant conditions should be comparable for each teacher.
> 2. Assign learners to teachers randomly.
> 3. More than one performance test should be completed by each teacher.
> 4. Preserve test security.

Earlier, we had identified these two procedures for using performance tests in instructional improvement:

> *For instructional improvement:*
> 1. Clinical observers should conduct instructional analyses based on learner performance.
> 2. Provide opportunities for replanning and reteaching of unsuccessful lessons.

Briefly review these two recommendations. Even earlier, we had treated five procedures recommended for both instructional improvement and skill assessment.

> *For instructional improvement and skill assessment:*
> 1. Allow sufficient planning time for the teacher.
> 2. Use naive but teachable learners.
> 3. Use small or large groups of learners.
> 4. Item sampling posttests may be used.
> 5. Routinely assess learner effect.

For practice in deciding whether certain procedures should be used for instructional improvement, skill assessment, or both, indicate, next to Number 9 on your answer sheet, whether each of these procedures should be used when performance tests are employed for instructional improvement (II), skill assessment (SA), or both (B).

9.
1. Clinical observers should conduct instructional analyses based on learner performance.
2. Use small or large groups of learners.

Procedure number one, performance-based analysis, is recommended for instructional improvement purposes, while procedure number two, involving flexible learner group size, is recommended for both instructional improvement and skill assessment purposes.

How about these next two procedures? Answer next to Number 10.

10.
1. Assign learners to teachers randomly.
2. Routinely assess learner affect.

Procedure one, randomized learner assignment, was recommended for skill assessment purposes, while procedure two, assessing learner affect, was recommended for both skill assessment and instructional improvement.

Let's close this program with two fictitious examples of educators using teaching performance tests, first for skill assessment and second for instructional improvement. Recalling all of the procedural recommendations we have been discussing, decide whether, in general, the educators are using performance tests properly. Examine Mr. Hill's use of teaching performance tests for *skill assessment* and decide whether he is generally following recommended procedures. Answer Yes or No next to Number 11.

11.
Mr. Hill directs a college teacher preparation program. To supply potential employers with useful selection data, he has each student teacher complete four comparable 20-minute performance tests with different randomly assigned groups of eight pupils. The objectives for the tests are based on novel subject matter and Mr. Hill maintains test security.

In general, Mr. Hill appears to be using teaching performance tests properly for skill assessment purposes. Data yielded by such performance tests would be valuable, along with other information, to prospective hiring officials. If routinely gathered each year, such data could also help Mr. Hill and his associates study the effectiveness of their teacher preparation program in helping prospective teachers increase their instructional skill.

For a final exercise, decide whether the elementary school teachers in this next example are, in general, following recommended procedures for using teaching performance tests for instructional improvement. Answer next to Number 12 on the answer sheet.

12.
All fifth-and sixth-grade teachers at P.S. 121 spend two days each week after school taking turns completing 30-minute performance tests in remedial reading for small groups of poor readers. After the posttest the teachers discuss the lesson in terms of posttest results. Unsuccessful lessons are redone in later weeks.

You should have answered Yes, for these teachers are quite effectively employing teaching performance tests for instructional improvement. On the basis of this activity the entire staff can probably become far more proficient in bringing about intended behavior changes in learners. Indeed, whether for skill assessment or instructional improvement, teaching performance tests can be a useful tool in the hands of the resourceful educator, for they provide a defensible index of the degree to which instructors can promote worthwhile changes in learners. And that, after all, is what teachers should be about.

Alternative Avenues to Educational Accountability

Objectives

This program is designed, in general terms, to expand the reader's range of alternatives regarding the meaning of educational accountability. The term "accountability," when applied to education, often conveys a too limited conception of the responsibility an educator is supposed to assume regarding the quality of his efforts. This program will show the reader three different strategies—personal, professional, and public—for implementing accountability strategies. Specifically, at the conclusion of the program the reader will be able to:

1. Describe the three forms of educational accountability treated in the program, that is, *personal, professional,* and *public* accountability.
2. Properly classify fictitious descriptions of alleged systems of educational accountability as (a) not a true accountability system, or an instance of (b) personal, (c) professional, or (d) public accountability.
3. Describe one major strength and one major weakness of each of the three forms of educational accountability.
4. Supply at least one new illustration of each of the three forms of educational accountability described in the program.

106

For American schools the 1970s may well be an era of *educational accountability.* Just what is educational accountability and how will it affect those in the educational community? Certainly the concept of accountability is referred to with greatly increasing frequency in the professional literature of education at meetings of educational organizations, and even in state and federal legislative assemblies. Yet, if we carefully inspect the rhetoric used to either promote or denigrate the idea of educational accountability, we discover that many people possess only a superficial understanding of what the expression means and how its implementation might alter educational practice. Accordingly, this program will describe three essentially different approaches to educational accountability and will offer specific illustrations of how each scheme might be implemented. Hopefully, by recognizing alternative methods of moving toward instructional systems based on somewhat varied conceptions of accountability, the educator can make a more enlightened choice regarding his own participation in schemes involving a commitment to educational accountability.

Let's turn first to a definition of the expression *educational accountability,* for although we shall examine three different methods of implementing systems of educational accountability, they all have one basic similarity: an assumption that those designing or implementing educational systems must become responsible for the results those systems produce in the intended learners. This responsibility is not discharged merely by *asserting* that the accountability-oriented educator is responsible but, rather, it requires that he produce *evidence* regarding the outcomes that have been produced in learners as a consequence of his instruction.

This evidence is then made available to different individuals, for the accountable educator accepts both positive and negative judgments of his instructional efforts and the subsequent actions which may stem from those judgments. Indeed, the fact that evidence regarding the results of instruction is de-

> "AFTER ALL, WE'RE PAYING FOR THE PLACE."

PRINCIPAL

ACCOUNTABILITY

manded by different groups or individuals permits distinctions to be drawn between alternative systems of educational accountability. Who is making the decision determines the kind of decisions which are made regarding an instructor's efforts. Let's examine three forms of educational accountability: *personal accountability, professional accountability,* and *public accountability.*

The key difference in each of these three forms of accountability is the nature of the decision maker who demands evidence regarding the outcomes of instruction. In the case of personal accountability, an instructor is the initiator of any review of the results of his own instruction. Others may be called in—for instance, one or more colleagues to participate in an instructional review—but it is the individual teacher who decides whether the review of his instructional results will be solitary or include others. For example, a teacher who carefully evaluates the kinds of changes in learners yielded by his instructional efforts, then makes decisions regarding the modification of his teaching tactics, is engaging in a form of personal educational accountability. No one else need be

involved in such decisions. In a well devised personal accountability scheme decisions regarding instructional modifications
are not capricious. Rather, the educational practitioner who is
personally accountable *systematically* amassed evidence regarding the good or bad results of his teaching and is prepared
to take the actions dictated by the evidence. If he consults
others regarding these activities, it is a totally individual decision.

Professional accountability, on the other hand, is initiated by
a group of the instructor's colleagues such as the faculty
members of his school or school district or perhaps his teachers' organization. The choice to review the results of instruction is not the individual teacher's to make. An element of
imposition is present in this form of accountability, but the
imposed demand for accountability emerges from within the
teaching profession, rather than from external quarters. Suppose, for example, that a high school faculty voted over-
whelmingly to set a system whereby each teacher would
have to produce tangible evidence of the kinds of learner
progress being made each month, such evidence to be re-
viewed by specially designated teachers representing the
subject field involved. The results would be made available
only among the faculty, with the primary purpose being to
identify and help to improve less effective instructors. This
would be an instance of professional educational accountability.

Public accountability, as might be inferred from its name,
occurs when the public demands evidence regarding the
quality of learner attainments—for instance, if the school
board requires that reasonably interpretable evidence of
learner achievement be supplied to school district taxpayers
each year so that laymen can reach results-based judgments
regarding the school system's effectiveness.

> *Different forms of educational accountability:*
> *Personal.* Teacher voluntarily initiates plan to review
> evidence of learner growth.

> *Professional.* A professional group requires evidence of learner growth.
> *Public.* The public or its representatives require evidence of learner growth.

To help you become more familiar with these three forms of educational accountability, we will now supply some fictitious illustrations of educational situations allegedly involving educational accountability. After examining the situation, decide first whether educational accountability is present at all, then, if it is, whether it is primarily a case of personal, professional, or public accountability. For this first answer, next to Number 1 on the answer sheet write personal, professional, public, or none.

1.

Mrs. Hein, a senior high school history teacher, spends many hours discussing alternative teaching techniques with her colleagues. Most of Mrs. Hein's reading time is taken up in an effort to discover innovative approaches to teaching history.

Although Mrs. Hein certainly seems well intentioned, you should have responded "none," for there is no indication that anyone is being guided by *evidence* regarding the *results* of instruction. Had Mrs. Hein and her colleagues weighed the value of alternative teaching tactics according to evidence based on what had happened to Mrs. Hein's students as a consequence of instruction, this would have been an instance of personal educational accountability. As it is, no educational accountability is implied in this situation. Instead, Mrs. Hein seems to be engaging in a particularly prevalent error of teachers: she has become enamoured of instructional innovation for its own sake and has failed to draw the crucial evaluation between *innovation* and *improvement.* Educational accountability requires us to display clear evidence that all innovative practices produce worthwhile results in learners.

Answer personal, professional, public, or none next to Number 2 on the answer sheet.

2.
Mr. Coe undertakes each teaching unit only after deciding on several measurable objectives and the levels of learner proficiency he wishes. Later, he survey learner performance and decides whether to modify the unit for subsequent classes.

Here we have a clear instance of personal educational accountability, for Mr. Coe is apparently gathering evidence regarding learner performance in order to make his own decisions regarding whether to alter his teaching tactics.

How about this next situation? Answer next to Number 3 whether these teachers are employing a personal, professional, or public accountability strategy.

3.
Three math teachers have voluntarily formed a teaching team for a remedial mathematics class. At the closing of each week the three teachers evaluate each other's efforts on the basis of their pupils' test performance.

This situation also reflects a case of personal educational accountability, for the three teachers are voluntarily involving their colleagues in an appraisal of their teaching activities based upon evidence of learner growth. No professional group or public representatives have demanded that the teachers share the evidence regarding their performance with anyone else; it was a voluntary act on the part of the teachers.

Ideally the three teachers would employ other indications of the new outcomes of the instruction, for example, indicators of the attitudes and interests their pupils were developing toward mathematics. In general, the more criteria we use in an educational accountability system, the better decisions we will be able to reach. What form of educational accountability, if any, is being employed in this next exercise? Write your answer in the space provided by Number 4.

4.

A local teachers' organization has set up a mandatory *Critique Service* whereby a small group of members secure pupil evidence regularly from a member's teaching, then analyze the teaching with the member and, if learner performance indicates, suggest possible modifications.

Here we have an instance of professional accountability, for the evidence regarding the results of instruction is demanded by professional colleagues. A number of teachers' organizations have indicated a desire to play a more forceful role in promoting instructional improvement within their ranks by devising systems of educational accountability in which all members are required to participate. Results of these systems are typically not made available to employers, for the essence of professional accountability is to upgrade the quality of professional expertise, but to carry on that upgrading *within* the profession. Many educational analysts believe that the chief thrust toward educational accountability must come from professional groups which, concerned about improving the quality of their members' efforts, will initiate rigorous self-regulatory systems.

In the next exercise do we see an instance of educational accountability and, if so, what kind? Answer next to Number 5.

5.
The district school board requires each school in the district to report semiannually on pupil progress as measured by standardized achievement tests. By comparing current with past results, the board is influenced regarding school budget expenditures.

Here we have a fairly clear example of public educational accountability. It is unfortunate that the school board members have decided to use standardized achievement tests, for such measuring devices, while perhaps better than nothing, are not well suited for use in any kind of accountability systems. Not only do standardized tests typically yield indicators which are too global to permit intelligent decision making, but they also are often insensitive to the very type of learner growth we are trying to measure. There are preferable measurement alternatives.

In reviewing these three avenues to educational accountability, the common dimension in each is a commitment on the part of the educator to assume responsibility for the results of instruction. Evidence regarding the impact of instruction on learners is systematically accumulated and then made available to one or more audiences. If the initiator of the evidence-appraisal scheme is oneself, then personal accountability is involved; if the initiators are colleagues, then professional accountability is present; if the initiators are lay citizens or their representatives, for example, the school board or the board's administrative officers, then public accountability is involved.

Each of these three forms of educational accountability carries with it the potential to improve the quality of education.

However, each of the three forms contains inherent strengths and weaknesses. Those who mindlessly lump these three varieties into the same accountability sack confuse the issue. Accordingly, we shall examine each of the three alternatives in more detail.

Turning first to personal accountability, how might it work? Clearly the focus in this approach is self-improvement. A teacher wants to get better at what he's doing and becomes

PERSONAL ACCOUNTABILITY
−a focus on self-improvement

personally liable for the changes he is producing or not producing in his students. Thus, for example, we might find a teacher who, prior to an instructional sequence, routinely establishes expected levels of learner proficiency. By comparing the actual levels of learner progress after instruction with the hoped-for progress, the teacher can reach a more defensible judgment regarding his instructional effectiveness. A personal system of educational accountability involves more than a casual "look-see" at the end of an instructional sequence, even if other teachers participate in the "look." Most teachers typically get a somewhat ill-defined impression of whether they have been teaching well. A true system of per-

sonal educational accountability involves the establishment
of a *systematic mechanism* whereby the instructor can appraise the quality of his efforts in terms of evidence regarding
learner growth.

For instance, a teacher might enter into a personal contract
with himself wherein he spells out in advance of instruction
the specific kinds of learner objectives he is trying to achieve
and the type of evidence he will use to indicate whether the
objectives have been attained. He can then routinely gather
the postinstruction evidence and see whether his objectives
have been achieved. Decisions on whether to modify the instructional sequence the next time it is taught or to modify
comparable sequences are made, in the main, on the basis of
the prestipulated evidence. A teacher might wish to retain a
consistent record of such contracts and their results, perhaps
planning to use such evidence in future interactions with supervisors, employing officials, etc.

Another approach a teacher might use to make assessments
of his own teaching skill are the recently devised *teaching
performance tests.* Briefly, such a test consists of one or more
specific measurable objectives designed to be accomplished
in a set period of time, perhaps 15 minutes or a single class
period. The performance test also contains any background
information necessary for the teacher to prepare a lesson
designed to accomplish the objective. A posttest is given to
the learners at the close of the lesson, but the posttest should
not be seen by the teacher until the lesson is concluded. The
pupils' performance on the posttest provides an index of the
teacher's skill in promoting prespecified changes in learners.
The results of such performance tests can obviously be used
by the instructor as he appraises the quality of his teaching.
For some performance tests there is information available
regarding how well other teachers have been able to do with
the test; a teacher can compare his own performance with
that of other instructors. Since this approach is a system of
personal accountability, however, it is the teacher's choice
whether to make such comparisons and, more fundamentally,

his decision whether to undertake any accountability system in the first place. He is, in a very real sense, accountable to himself for the results he secures with learners.

> *Personal accountability*
> *Strength:* Its voluntary nature and privacy possibilities encourage teacher participation.
> *Weakness:* Less competent teachers may not voluntarily set up an accountability program.

This very feature of personal educational accountability is at the same time its most prominent strength and its greatest weakness. Since the teacher is the exclusive initiator of the system and, if he wishes, he can be the sole examiner of evidence of pupil performance, the approach is obviously not very threatening. As a consequence, many teachers should be willing to employ it. On the other hand, since personal accountability schemes are essentially volitional and often private, the instructors who most need to improve themselves may be the least likely to engage in such approaches. For the weak teacher, even a private mirroring of his mediocrity is not pleasant. Thus, we can identify a major strength and weakness of personal educational accountability.

After studying for a moment, see if you can recall the strength and weakness of personal accountability we have just described by listing each next to Number 6 on the answer sheet.

6.
Personal accountability
Strength:
Weakness:

Compare your answer to the strength and weakness listed earlier. Let's turn to professional educational accountability,

for while this less private form of accountability fails to capitalize on the chief strength of a personal accountability system, it does correct a major weakness of the personal
approach to educational accountability. The distinguishing
feature of a professional accountability system is that it is
initiated by a group of professionals such as a teachers' organization. Assuming it has the power to implement its plan, if
the professional group requires teacher participation in the enterprise, then teachers *have* to participate whether they wish to
or not. This departure from the completely volitional nature of
personal accountability obviously makes professional accountability more threatening for many teachers. On the positive
side, the possibility that incompetent teachers could avoid participating in the system is eliminated by requiring their involve-
ment.

TEACHER'S ASSOCIATION
MUDD VALLEY SCHOOL DISTRICT

PROFESSIONAL ACCOUNTABILITY
a collegial improvement scheme

Let's look at some examples of how a professional accountability system might work. One clear illustration would arise
if the local teachers' organization set up a mandatory scheme
for monitoring its members' instructional prowess. Suppose,

for instance, that the teachers' organization required its members to participate in semiannual teaching performance tests clinics whereby all teachers completed several half-hour teaching performance tests using randomly assigned small groups of learners. Based on results of the performance tests, those members most in need of instructional assistance could be subsequently aided by a special improvement task force set up by the teachers' organization. This operation would be required of all, but would be a totally internal professional enterprise. The professional group would be trying to improve its own expertise via a system of collegial support. Results would not be made available to school administrators or the public.

Consider another variation on the professional accountability theme. The members of an English department in a junior high school might vote to set up a systematic mechanism for monitoring the quality of each other's instruction. Every month each teacher would write at least two goals he would attempt to accomplish during the succeeding month and the evidence which would reflect the attainment of those goals. While most teachers have other goals they wish to pursue, the two selected should be considered important by each teacher.

These goal-plus-evidence statements could then be filed with the elected department chairman who was also commissioned to appoint one teacher to help every other teacher in the collection of the evidence at the close of the month. At that time the evidence could be collected and shared during several after-school faculty meetings in which the teachers could trade insights as to why certain instructional tactics seemed effective or ineffective in relationship to the evidence of goal attainment.

The teachers might or might not decide to involve the school administration in their activities; in some situations the supervision resources of a district are considerable and the teachers might wish to capitalize on them. The important point is that it is the *teachers* who decide whether to initiate the accountability system in the first place and, after doing so, decide with whom the evidence regarding learner growth should be shared.

> *Professional accountability*
> *Strength:* Its intraprofessional nature, though non-voluntary, is less threatening.
> *Weakness:* Members of a professional group may be inclined to shield the less effective colleagues.

In examining the merits of professional accountability we see immediately that since it is an intraprofessional operation it would be less threatening to many teachers, even though required of all. This is its major strength and represents the reason why a number of educators believe professional organizations may lead the way in implementing educational accountability systems. On the negative side, professional associations have historically been reluctant to expose or expel their ineffective members. Thus, even if the professional group is unable to improve certain of its members' skills, they may not be willing to make the hard decision to reassign or even release a weak member.

To fix these strength and weakness points more firmly for yourself, study them for a moment, then see if you can, in your own words, write them alongside Number 7 in the answer sheet without referring to the text.

7.
Professional accountability
Strength:
Weakness:

Check your answer against the strength and weakness listed in the text.

Turning to public accountability, we find that citizens may act, typically through their elected representatives such as school board members or legislators, to require a system of educational accountability.

PUBLIC ACCOUNTABILITY

For example, suppose a state legislature enacts a law requiring all districts in the state to choose one of several alternative schemes (devised by the legislature) for annually releasing to the public evidence regarding the results of instruction. Such a system is clearly an instance of a public accountability scheme, the effectiveness of which would depend on the quality of the procedures worked out by the legislature.

Or suppose a school board requires its administrative staff to secure systematic evidence regarding the attainment of a number of explicit objectives which the local community has identified as important. This too would be an instance of public educational accountability.

> *Public accountability*
> *Strength:* Full and open evidence is available to all regarding effective and ineffective instruction.

> *Weakness:* The education profession may marshall sufficient resistance to make an accountability system ineffectual.

The chief advantage of a public accountability approach is that because it is imposed from the outside on the educator there is less likelihood that instances of ineffective instruction will be tolerated. And since all forms of educational accountability are designed to improve the quality of instruction the students receive, that is clearly a dividend. On the other hand, since imposed from without, many teachers will resist public accountability schemes with a vengeance. Some will resist because they have basic doubts regarding the wisdom of such approaches. Some will resist because of personal fears, for surely the individual most terrified by a full blown accountability system is the person unable to promote demonstrable growth in learners. It is also not difficult to imagine poorly conceptualized public accountability systems operated by ill-informed or politically repressive individuals. Some people, fearing such misuses of a system, may resist all accountability schemes.

After briefly reviewing them, see if you can describe, in your own words, the strength and weakness of the public accountability systems we have been describing without referring to the text. Answer next to Number 8.

8.
Public accountability
Strength:
Weakness:

Compare your answer with the strength and weakness listed earlier.

Even though an attempt has been made to distinguish among alternative approaches to educational accountability on the basis of who initiates the demand for evidence regarding instructional quality, these distinctions don't always hold up quite so clearly in the real world. It is certainly possible to blend one or more of these alternatives into an effective accountability system. You should attempt to devise innovative ways of implementing each of the three forms of accountability described in the program. If possible, at the close of the program spend some time trying to generate new variations of each of the three accountability approaches. You might also consider other strengths and weaknesses of such schemes.

Many educational evaluators believe that educational accountability systems offer immense promise for improving the quality of our educational system. By thinking more intensively about the types of educational accountability treated in this program, perhaps you can decide whether you share this belief. If you do, of course, then the next step is to devise and implement the best system of educational accountability that you can.

Program
Answer
Sheets

Current Conceptions of Educational Evaluation *Answer Sheet*

1. Grading/Evaluation
2. Evaluation/Research
3. Measurement/Evaluation
4. Measurement/Evaluation
5. Measurement/Evaluation
6. Formative/Summative
7. Formative/Summative
8. Formative/Summative
9. Process/Product
10. Process/Product
11. Process/Product
12. Assessment of merit/Aid to decision makers
13. Assessment of merit/Aid to decision makers

Modern Measurement Methods *Answer Sheet*

1. C   N
2. C   N
3. C   N
4. C   N
5. _____
   _____
   _____
   _____
6. _____
   _____
   _____
7. C   N
8. C   N
9. C   N
10. C   N
11. C   N
12. C   N
13. C   N
14. C   N

Instructional Supervision: A Criterion-Referenced
Strategy *Answer Sheet*

1. Yes   No
2. (1) _____
   (2) _____
   (3) _____
   (4) _____
3. Yes   No
4. Yes   No
5. Yes   No
6. Yes   No
7. Yes   No
8. (1) _____
   (2) _____
   (3) _____
   (4) _____
9. (1) _____
   (2) _____
10. Yes   No
11. Yes   No
12. Yes   No
13. Yes   No
14. Yes   No

Constructing Teaching Performance Tests *Answer Sheet*

1. (1) _____
   (2) _____
   (3) _____
2. (1) _____
   (2) _____
   (3) _____
3. A   B
4. A   B   C   D
5. A   B   C
6. A   B   C   D
7. Yes   No
8. A   B   C
9. A   B   C
10. (1) _____
    (2) _____
    (3) _____
    (4) _____
    (5) _____
11.   _____
       _____
       _____
       _____
       _____
12.   _____
       _____

Using Teaching Performance Tests *Answer Sheet*

(II = Instructional Improvement, SA = Skill Assessment)

1. II   SA
2. II   SA
3. II   SA
4. II   SA
5. (1) _____
   _____
   (2) _____
   _____
6. (1) _____
   (2) _____
   (3) _____
   (4) _____
   (5) _____
7. Yes   No
8. Yes   No
9. (1) II   SA   B
   (2) II   SA   B
10. (1) II   SA   B
    (2) II   SA   B
11. Yes   No
12. Yes   No

Alternative Avenues to Educational Accountability
Answer Sheet

1. _____

2. _____

3. _____

4. _____

5. _____

6. (a) _____

    _____

   (b) _____

    _____

7. (a) _____

    _____

   (b) _____

    _____

8. (a) _____

    _____

   (b) _____

    _____

Mastery
Tests

Mastery Test: Current Conceptions of Educational Evaluation

Name _____

Part I. Designate, by placing the appropriate letter in the space before each item, whether the following individuals are engaged primarily in *measurement* (write an *A*) or *evaluation*
(write a *B*).

_____ 1. Mr. Field, a district guidance supervisor, has been
asked to supply a complete breakdown of the district
pupils' reading achievement status. Accordingly, he secures scores for each pupil on a nationally standardized reading achievement test, then presents the
median and mean score for each grade level in each
school in the district.

_____ 2. A school principal has been observing each teacher's
classroom instruction and, on the basis of a carefully
constructed observation schedule, rates each teacher
as "below average," "average," or "above average."

_____ 3. Mrs. Kline, a sixth-grade teacher, gives weekly math-
emathics quizzes to her pupils and returns the scored
papers to the class in terms of percentage right answers for each pupil.

_____ 4. An educational psychologist compares the effectiveness of two different methods of teaching children
how to read graphs. He employs a careful randomized
assignment pretest–posttest two group design and dis-
cerns, via a *t* test analysis, that one method is 42
percent more effective than the other in promoting
posttest growth, a difference which is significant
beyond the .001 level of confidence.

_____ 5. A school curriculum committee examines the currently
used textbooks in the district and decides that their
content is, on a 10 point scale of "current relevance,"
only a 3. Thus, they conclude the text content is out-
moded.

Part II. Designate, by placing the appropriate letter in the spaces
before each item, whether the following individuals are engaged primarily in *formative evaluation* (write an *A*) or *summative evaluation* (write a *B*).

_____ 6. A former major league first baseman, and currently coach of the local high school baseball team, "Stretch" Marx, keeps an intense daily record of how his players hit different kinds of pitches, e.g., curves and fast balls. At the close of the day he identifies the three worst hitters on each type of pitch, then gives them a different form of batting practice for the last 15 minutes of the practice period.

_____ 7. The state textbook selection committee chooses between three competing spelling primers for statewide adoption.

_____ 8. A developer of programmed instructional materials tests his preliminary versions of all programs with small groups of learners, then revises the programs on the basis of learner performance.

_____ 9. A writer of educational textbooks sends early versions of his manuscripts to teacher friends who critique each chapter. Then the writer uses their comments to revise his manuscript.

_____ 10. At the close of the school year Mr. Smith gives his biology class the same exam he has given every class for the past five years. He compares each new group with previous groups to give himself an idea of how well he has been teaching that year.

Part III. Designate, by placing the appropriate letter in the space before each item, whether the following individuals are evaluating primarily by employing *process criteria* (write an *A*) or *product criteria* (write a *B*).

_____ 11. Miss Werdsa Minet, local typing teacher, judges her own teaching prowess largely in terms of how many practice minutes the pupils are able to have each day after preliminary paper distribution and roll call activities are concluded.

_____ 12. A regional accrediting association judges schools in terms of their library facilities and the graduate education records of their faculty.

_____ 13. High school faculty members receive salary increases in relationship to the number of inservice workshops they have attended.

_____ 14. A school district appraises its annual effectiveness in relationship to how well learners perform at the close of the year on district-wide achievement examinations.

_____ 15. Mrs. Harris, an American history teacher, evaluates her own teaching proficiency according to how well students like history, as reflected by their anonymous responses to an interest questionnaire.

Part IV. Designate, by placing the appropriate letter in the space before each item, whether the following individuals are engaged primarily in *evaluation as an assessment of merit* (write an *A*) or *evaluation as an aid to decision making* (write a *B*).

_____ 16. An evaluation consultant supplies information to the local board that, in his view, the current goals of the district's curriculum are "trivial."

_____ 17. In an effort to determine what goals should be pursued by the local school system, an evaluator discusses specific goal preferences of different groups in the community, e.g., parents, children, businessmen, then presents their dissimilar perceptions to the administrators of the school.

_____ 18. A school superintendent describes school-by-school test results in his district for the board of education, then presents national normative data for similar school systems in order that the board members may contrast local performance with national performance.

_____ 19. Because they must choose a set of instructional materials for the district's new drug education programs, the district curriculum committee secures the services of an evaluation consultant who compiles an exhaustive array of descriptive data, e.g., cost and field test results, on the four sets of materials under consideration.

_____ 20. After examining his history pupils' end-of-unit test scores, Mr. Wilson concludes that they performed well below what they should have and, consequently, that his instruction was deficient.

Mastery Test: Modern Measurement Methods

Name _____

Part I.

1. In brief, describe the principal purpose of norm-referenced testing.
2. In brief, describe the principal purpose of criterion-referenced testing.

Part II. Directions: Identify by placing a *C* or *N* before the item whether each of the following operations is more appropriate for criterion-referenced *(C)* or norm-referenced *(N)* testing.

_____ 3. Use of judges to determine the validity of test items, that is, the degree to which the items are consonant with the objectives.

_____ 4. Reporting scores in terms of percentiles.

_____ 5. Using item analysis procedures to identify and eliminate nondiscriminating items.

_____ 6. Designing test items so that they produce maximum score variability.

_____ 7. Revising the test until it yields an internal consistency reliability coefficiency of at least .85.

_____ 8. Reporting scores in terms of "percent of items correct."

Part III. Directions: In the same manner (by placing a *C* or *N* in front of the item) indicate whether the following measuring devices would be more suitable for criterion-referenced measurement or norm-referenced measurement.

_____ 9. A 30-item multiple choice examination which accurately reflects the instructional objective on which it was based. The test is used by a teacher to measure whether a particular segment of a course is effective.

_____ 10. A test of academic aptitude used for predicting one's college grade point average.

_____ 11. A nationally standardized group I.Q. test.

_____ 12. A pregnancy test.

_____ 13. This test is used each year to identify the upper 10 percent (in academic achievement) of a high school's graduating seniors so that they can be considered for scholarships at the nearby state college.

_____ 14. Tests constituted by item sampling to measurement achievement of course goals.

Part IV. _Directions:_ Respond in the same manner to the following items. Do these measurement situations seem to require a criterion-referenced or norm-referenced measurement?

_____ 15. You wish to select those pupils in a group of third-grade children who have mastered a given set of mathematical skills so that they can be admitted to a new enrichment program. There is no limit on number of students who can be admitted to the new program.

_____ 16. You wish to develop a short programmed text which accomplishes three specific objectives. You need to build a test to measure the objectives—and, therefore, whether the text was successful.

_____ 17. You are a first-grade teacher who suddenly has available five well-trained tutors from the district high school. You are anxious to construct a test which will identify the 10 least able readers so that the tutors can work with them.

_____ 18. You want to build a test to help you determine how well you have been teaching your college history course.

_____ 19. You want to build a test which will identify the 40 pupils in your school who have the most positive attitude toward teaching minority groups.

Part V.

20. In a few sentences, describe the basic procedure for constituting a test by means of item sampling.

Mastery Test: Instructional Supervision:
A Criterion-Referenced Strategy

Name _____

Part I.

1. In the spaces provided, describe the two primary functions of an instructional supervisor who uses a criterion-referenced strategy.
   (A) _____
   (B) _____

Part II.

2. For each of these two functions, list four recommended activities of a criterion-referenced instructional supervisor.
   A. (1) _____
      (2) _____
      (3) _____
      (4) _____
   B. (1) _____
      (2) _____
      (3) _____
      (4) _____

Part III. *Directions:* For the following items, place an *X* before each which describes a supervisory action and/or decision which is *consistent* with a criterion-referenced strategy.

_____ 3. The district supervisor observes a fourth-grade teacher's class for several days, then recommends that the teacher attempt to have more of the children respond actively to instructional stimuli. The supervisor contends that too few youngsters are responding during the conduct of instructional activities.

_____ 4. A supervising teacher in a junior high school English class notes that her student teacher does not immediately confirm whether student responses to his questions are correct or incorrect. She urges him to provide immediate knowledge of results, but to do so with tact.

_____ 5. After learning from a conversation with one of the new teachers in his district that she is extremely nondirective in conducting her eighth-grade classes, Mr. James, the social studies supervisor, strongly advises that she modify her approach. While perhaps suitable for older learners, he urges that 14-year-old children need much more direction from the teacher.

_____ 6. Mr. Versey, an elementary supervisor, always commences a supervisory conference by asking the teacher to identify the instructional goals he has for his pupils.

_____ 7. On the basis of discussions with a number of other teachers, the district supervisor reaches a negative judgment regarding the instructional proficiency of Miss Hill, a first-year teacher. Well over half of her colleagues, as well as the principal, consider Miss Hill to be a poor instructor.

_____ 8. This supervisor spends a great deal of time working with a teacher in identifying his instructional objectives and making them more worthwhile. The supervisor and the teacher discuss with colleagues the merit of particular objectives and try to improve those objectives which others suggest are deficient.

_____ 9. Mr. Carlton, a science supervisor in the elementary grades, spends most of his time determining whether the instructional objectives which teachers have identified are being accomplished by learners. He does, however, spend a good segment of his efforts on learners. For example, he tries to talk with students to determine how interested they are in the general field of science.

_____ 10. Mrs. Peters has acquired a number of interesting approaches to the teaching of English usage. In her relations with the teachers she supervises, she offers suggestions regarding these techniques. The teachers are constantly amazed by the variety of suggestions she has regarding instructional procedures.

Mastery Test: Constructing Teaching Performance Tests

Name _____

1. Briefly describe the rationale underlying the use of teaching performance tests as a measure of instructional skill.

2. Briefly describe the four steps involved in conducting a teaching performance test.

3. List five attributes of a well-constructed teaching performance test.

Mastery Test: Using Teaching Performance Tests

Name _____

1. Briefly describe the two chief roles of teaching performance tests.

2. Indicate whether teaching performance tests should be used for *instructional improvement* (II) or *skill assessment* (SA) in the following selections.

_____ a. To make decisions regarding tenure.

_____ b. To help a teacher increase his skill in accomplishing prespecified objectives.

_____ c. To evaluate the quality of inservice teacher education programs.

_____ d. To help a departmental faculty become better instructors.

_____ e. To make differentiated staffing assignments.

3. Indicate with an II, SA, or B whether each of the following procedures is recommended for instructional improvement, skill assessment, or both.

_____ a. Preserve test security.

_____ b. More than one performance test should be completed by each teacher.

_____ c. Use small or large groups of learners.

_____ d. Provide opportunities for replanning and reteaching of unsuccessful lessons.

_____ e. Use naive but teachable students.

4. What, if anything, is wrong with the way Mr. Jones is using teaching performance tests? Answer in the space below the item.

> Mr. Jones wishes to judge which of three student teachers assigned to his twelfth-grade world history class is the best. He can retain one of the student teachers next semester as part of a newly constituted teaching team. He has each student teacher select six children from the class and then gives them 15 minutes to prepare to teach a 20-minute performance test regarding a little known phase of European history. After the lessons are finished, the posttest results are used by Mr. Jones to make the decision regarding which student teacher to retain.

Mastery Test: Alternative Avenues to Educational Accountability

Name _____

I.   Briefly describe the following three forms of educational accountability:

(a)   *Personal*

(b)   *Professional*

(c)   *Public*

II.   For each of the following fictitious descriptions indicate by supplying the appropriate letter (a, b, c, or d) whether the description should be classified as:
    a: Not a true accountability system.
    b: Personal educational accountability.
    c: Professional educational accountability.
    d: Public educational accountability.

_____   1.   The district school superintendent initiates a mandatory scheme to secure annual achievement test performance from each mathematics teacher's class, summary data being given thereafter to the school board.

_____   2.   Mr. Smith always tries to attend to the results his instruction has on learners insofar as they offer anonymous end-of-course evaluation of the quality of the course and of his instructional efforts.

_____   3.   Miss Smith selects one major objective for each month of the academic year and administers an examination based on each objective to her students. She calculates summary statistics on the test results, then discusses any particularly poor results with her colleagues to secure suggestions for improvements.

_____   4.   The local teachers' organization requires its members to keep anecdotal records regarding the general kinds of instructional activities they engage in each year.

_____   5.   A high school science faculty votes to require monthly criterion tests of all pupils, then contrast these for each faculty member to locate those who need special help.

III. Describe, in brief, one strength and one weakness of each of the following forms of educational accountability:

1. *Personal*

   Strength:

   Weakness:

2. *Professional*

   Strength:

   Weakness:

3. *Public*

   Strength:

   Weakness:

IV. Supply one new illustration (one not treated in the program) of each of the following forms of educational accountability: personal, professional, and public.

Answers to
Mastery
Tests

Current Conceptions of Educational Evaluation

Part I.
1. A, 2. B, 3. A, 4. A, 5. B.

Part II.
6. A, 7. B, 8. A, 9. A, 10. B.

Part III.
11. A, 12. A, 13. A, 14. B, 15. B.

Part IV.
16. A, 17. B, 18. B, 19. B, 20. A.

Modern Measurement Methods

Part I.
1. To ascertain an individual's performance in relationship to the performance of others on the same measuring device.
2. To ascertain an individual's performance with respect to an established criterion, i.e., performance scale.

Part II.
3. C, 4. N, 5. N, 6. N, 7. N, 8. C.

Part III.
9. C, 10. N, 11. N, 12. C, 13. N, 14. C.

Part IV.
15. C, 16. C, 17. N, 18. C, 19. N.

Part V.
20. Different individuals complete different parts of the test, their combined performances yielding an estimate of the total group performance on the test.

Instructional Supervision: A
Criterion-Referenced Strategy

Part I.
1. A. Help the teacher select more defensible educational objectives.
   B. Help the teacher achieve the instructional objectives.

Part II.
2. A. (1) Identify any curricular constraints.
      (2) State all objectives operationally.
      (3) Consider alternative objectives.
      (4) Evaluate and decide on each potential objective.
   B. (1) Determines the teacher's objectives.
      (2) Secures evidence regarding their achievement.
      (3) Looks for undesirable side effects.
      (4) Suggests alternative procedures for unachieved objectives.

Part III.
An *X* should be placed only before items 6, 8, and 9.

Constructing Teaching Performance Tests

1. By having teachers pursue a common objective, their abilities to accomplish a prespecified instructional objective can be assessed.
2. 1. The teacher is given the objective(s) and necessary background information.
   2. The teacher plans the lesson.
   3. The teacher conducts the lesson.
   4. The learners are posttested.
3. 1. The objective must be measurable and attainable in the time available.
   2. The objective should be unfamiliar to the learner but not seen as absurd.
   3. Background information for the teacher should be adequate but brief.
   4. Measurement procedures should be congruent with the objective and easy to administer.
   5. The test must be able to discriminate among teachers.

Using Teaching Performance Tests

1. 1. To improve one's teaching proficiency, that is, for *instruction improvement.*
   2. To measure one's instructional competence, that is, *skill assessment.*
2. a. SA, b. II, c. SA, d. II, e. SA.
3. a. SA, b. SA, c. B, d. II, e. B.
4. 1. Learners were not assigned randomly.
   2. Sufficient planning time was not allowed.
   3. More than one performance test per teacher should have been used.

Alternative Avenues to Educational Accountability

I. (a) Teacher voluntarily initiates plan to review evidence of learner growth.
   (b) A professional group requires evidence of learner growth.
   (c) The public or its representatives require evidence of learner growth.

II. 1. d, 2. a, 3. b, 4. a, 5. c.

III. 1. *Strength:* Its voluntary nature and privacy possibilities encourage teacher participation.
     Weakness: Less competent teachers may not voluntarily set up an accountability procedure.
   2. *Strength:* Its intraprofessional nature, though nonvoluntary, is less threatening.
     Weakness: Members of a professional group may be inclined to shield their less effective colleagues.
   3. *Strength:* Full and open evidence is available to all regarding effective and ineffective instruction.
     Weakness: The education profession may marshall sufficient resistance to make an accountability system ineffectual.

IV. Answers should be both novel and consistent with the general points identified above in response to question I.

MICHIGAN CHRISTIAN COLLEGE LIBRARY
ROCHESTER, MICH.

ENNIS AND NANCY HALL LIBRARY
ROCHESTER COLLEGE
800 WEST AVON ROAD
ROCHESTER HILLS, MI 48307